Dedication

To my younger self. Here's what I wish we'd known.

Acknowledgement

In thanks to my mom, Lia, and Geoff. You guys create the best team I could have asked for.

The Human Experience

VOLUME I

WHAT IS THE HUMAN EXPERIENCE?

Rae Beecher

Copyright © 2021 Rae Beecher

ISBN #: 978-1-7367228-0-0 (Paperback)
ISBN #: 978-1-7367228-1-7 (EPUB)

Library of Congress Control Number: 2021905058

All rights reserved. This book or any portion thereof may not be reproduced or used in any manner whatsoever without the express written permission of the publisher except for the use of brief quotations. If utilizing brief quotations reference of the author and work is necessary and cannot be utilized in a manner that indicates or implies Rae Beecher's endorsement or otherwise involvement in the work.

The content of this book is meant to expose and educate the reader. In no way does it replace diagnosis and treatment by a qualified medical practitioner or therapist. No expressed or implied guaranteed results or improvement from the use of the recommendations and information can be given or liability taken.

Editing by Lia Ottaviano.
Cover & Book Design by Geoff Borin.
(The sacred geometric symbol found on the cover and within this book is known as the seed of life and has existed for centuries.)

Printed by Lightning Source LLC in the United States of America.

First printing edition 2021.

Publisher: Rae Medicine Woman LLC
PO Box 69
Oroville, WA
98844

www.raemedicinewoman.com

CONTENTS

Prologue
7

PART ONE
Why We Need A Personal Philosophy
15

PART TWO
My Personal Philosophy
52

PART THREE
The Human Experience – Life As I Understand It
79

PART FOUR
Your Personal Philosophy
107

Epilogue
149

PROLOGUE

Take a deep breath with me…

In…

Feel your lungs expand as the air seeps deep within your being.

Out…

The powerful force of your body, expelling this air.

And in…

Take a minute with me and just breathe. Go ahead, set a timer for one minute and just breathe.…

Now turn the page.

You spent an entire minute just breathing. Maybe you spent it thinking that the author of this book is totally nuts. Or you might have created a to-do list in your head. Or maybe, you seeped into your seat, closed your eyes, and spent an entire minute in peace.

You might be wondering what the purpose of this exercise was, so let me explain myself.

In asking you to just breathe for a single minute, I had you:

- Live in the moment.
- Slow down your life.
- Realize that your life can be slowed down.
- Realize that you are important, special, and precious to this world.

Within the pages of this book, you are cherished just because you breathe. You don't need money, status, or great wisdom to be loved. Within the pages of this book, the crazy author (me) has created a safe and loving environment.

No matter where you are in life, we are going to take a healing journey. Together.

The outcome is a thriving human experience. What I mean by this is that we will work to transform your life so that the loving and safe environment that you experience within the pages of this book will expand into every facet of your life.

A life where you will be able to thrive. A human experience where you will find healing, love, and happiness. Where you will learn to heal from the pain you encounter in life, rather than live a life where you manifest pain. A life where you feel safe and loved.

Let's get started.

PROLOGUE

I didn't start out searching for answers to life. I started out as a child in pain. Even though I have a loving mother and live safely in a wonderful country, I had pain. I had dysfunction.

This pain and dysfunction became a barrier in life that held me back from my dreams. It held me back from all the wonderful possibilities that can be found here on Earth, and as a result, life was less than I imagined it could be.

When I entered the 6th grade I began a journey that led me to a startling discovery: I cared what other people thought about me. By leaving my small Montessori school and entering the public school setting, I was no longer accepted as the unique duck I always had been.

With this one piece of dysfunctional information—the idea that what others think matters more than myself—I rewrote my whole life. I rewrote who I was. I went from dressing in clothes that I felt good in to saying and acting in ways that were like my peers, but not authentic to me. All to be accepted in this new environment.

This transformation I underwent was subtle, for the dysfunction I had was hidden. Cloaked as truths; buried deep within my subconscious. I was oblivious at first to the path I had veered onto.

I knew something wasn't right by my 6th grade graduation. It was like that spidery feeling on the back of your neck. But without a conscious answer to the dysfunction at play, I continued my life down that path.

As I entered middle school, I continued to sink deeper and deeper into the ways and actions of my peers, until one day I took a moment to look around me. What I saw was a reflection of the current me. I had found my problem.

I had strayed far away from the core of who I was, turning ruder and harsher than was my nature. It was in this moment of realization that I thought, "How did I get here?"

By the 8th grade I was fully aware that there was a problem. A problem that had only pulled me farther away from myself in the past two years. But even though I knew I had a problem I was oblivious as to how to fix it. So, while I thought about my predicament, I continued down that dysfunctional path, pulling farther from myself and all the happiness that I had imagined possible.

This is when I decided to do something about the situation I was in. I decided to go and hunt myself down. For I had reached a place where I was no longer certain about anything.

I felt like I knew nothing. I didn't even know if my favorite color was still the same. Something had to be done.

After I made this decision, I panicked. Not because I was worried about the dysfunction that I was going to get rid of. But because I had no clue what to do.

I was in pain and I wanted to do something about it. For myself, for hope, and for that kernel of self-love I had. So, I chose to turn around, face my problem, look it in the eye, and do something. I just didn't know what.

What followed was a long journey in search of me. In winging it.

It's been almost ten years since I entered the 6th grade. In that time, I have learned a lot about life and about people. I have gathered and collected this information like a blind man collects colors.

In my collection of knowledge, I have come to learn that life is all that I imagined it to be and more. I now know what it means to be a human being and have a human experience. Not just a surviving human experience, but one where we heal, love, discover happiness, and thus thrive.

The goal of a thriving human experience requires us to learn and understand life. To make changes and follow certain steps. In this way we build that thriving world, accomplishing our dreams. I call this progression of steps our healing journey. It is where we heal from all the wounds and roadblocks that keep us from life's possibilities and start living that life we at one time dreamed was real.

Components of a Healing Journey

One of the main triggers for my healing journey was the differences between my life and the lives of my peers and my favorite characters. Whether it was the latest book I was reading, a friend, or stranger, I discovered that they saw the world differently than I did.

Upon reflection, I wondered if this difference in sight and understanding is what led me to a life of pain and others to a life of adventure. Was it merely luck, or was there something I could be actively doing to help things change? Did I possess a power I didn't know I had?

It was from these many contemplative moments that I discovered that we each have created a personal philosophy.

> **PERSONAL PHILOSOPHY:**
> A guidebook that addresses the human experience, how the world works, and how we weave within the world.

We craft our personal philosophy by answering questions such as, "What is reality?" What is the nature of life?" "How do I weave into the world?" "Why am I here?"

From these conclusions and pieces of understanding, we shape a human experience. Influenced by what we know of the human experience and the tools we use, we create a rulebook that is our personal guidebook to life.

We build this rulebook as we grow and live in this world. We then take this rulebook and apply it to every area of our life. We utilize it each day as we make decisions and choices.

This means that our personal philosophy is directly linked to the quality of our human experience.

Except that we each carry with us false wisdom:

- From the teachings of adults in our lives.
- From the stories and lessons other children shared with us in childhood.
- From society and our culture.
- From our own incorrect hypothesis.
- From our understanding of life and the experiences we have had.

It was in this way, that I ended up taking a different path. So, as my path led me into a life of pain, it led others to a life of adventure and happiness. All based upon our understanding of how life works.

Each of us have built our current "reality" or truth based upon our understanding of life. But if our understanding is wrong, we can build a life where we care what other people think about us. We can live in chronic pain. We can be stuck just surviving, never truly thriving.

The plus side of this, is that human beings possess a power I didn't know we had. This power provides us the ability to change paths, all by updating our understanding of how life works.

Because our personal philosophy is essential, I believe that we need to do all we can to make sure that our personal philosophy is as healthy and happy as possible. That way, our life can be as healthy and happy as possible—it thus becomes a thriving human experience. So, rather than just accepting our current personal philosophy, let's inspect it and modify it. Let's put it to the test.

The focus of this book revolves around the human experience—what life is like, how it works, and the possibilities we have available to us as human beings. These basic truths that create a human experience will become the bedrock of our personal philosophy. Which will help us reach a place where we can actively choose what our life will be like.

Let the kernel of hope and self-love you have strengthen you so that you can face your dysfunction, look it in the eye, and work with me as I share with you the tools you need to eradicate it.

Work with me as we take this healing journey together. You do not walk alone.

PART 1

Why We Need A Personal Philosophy

I cared at one time-
  -what they thought
  -and if they'd mind

I cared who saw-
  -the spirit that I carry
  -the Spirit that I follow

I cared for my heart-
  -as if they might be able to break it
  -as if I might die

I care now-
  -for who I am
  -for what I know

I care for others-
  -they don't have to agree
  -but I can still help thee

I care-
  -because that's just me

Waiting on love is like waiting for air. Rather than waiting until you and your life match your dream, take a minute to breathe. Breathe with me, filling your body with the essential components to a happy life.

Love is not contingent on body type, status, wealth, or accomplishments. Just as a child is loved with its first breath and not its first word, love yourself with your first breath. Choose to love right now, before we even get into the first stage of this healing journey.

Philosophia: The Love of Wisdom

I chose to start our journey with the academic world of philosophy because while the journey we are taking might be new for you, you're not the first person to question life's possibilities. Many people all over the world, for centuries, have started their journey with philosophy.

Philosophers such as Socrates, Descartes, Plato, and Aristotle took nothing for granted. They reanalyzed all they thought they knew in an effort to understand the world.

From their new and improved understanding, they were able to craft a rulebook about the nature of reality that supported and guided them, rather than one that introduced pain and held them back. Thus, connecting them to the possibilities of life and a thriving human experience.

Philosophy was first coined by Pythagoras (570-495 BCE) and has only grown to this day. It just goes to show us that the questions concerning life and human nature are big and important to all of us.

Philosophy started with the purpose of studying anything. Philosophers spent their days searching for the answers to some of life's biggest questions.

- Who am I?
- Why am I here?
- What is the nature of reality?

Basically, how does the world work, and how do I work within the world? At its heart, philosophers strive to understand life and the human experience. Sound familiar?

So rather than taking this journey alone, we can take it together, utilizing the information others have learned before us. This will help our experience to be easier, happier, and safer.

As philosophers tackle the big questions, we are going to utilize their tools to create a healthy personal philosophy. From this personal philosophy, we will address those big philosophical questions. My goal is that by the end of this book, you will have a greater understanding of...

- What it means to be human.
- How life works and how we work with life.
- How we can go about creating that thriving human experience.

In this way, we'll uncover the tools, perceptions, rules, and answers that will support us as we flourish in life.

The Focus of Philosophy

Philosophy is not about being right or wrong. Rather, it is about our application of knowledge and our time spent thinking, considering, pondering, and reaching conclusions about life. In this way, we formulate an outline, our rulebook.

Since philosophy is not about being right, but about establishing answers and understanding, we are entering a world of discussion, or a dialectic.

> ### DIALECTIC:
> "[The] discussion and reasoning by dialogue as a method of intellectual investigation."
>
> Merriam Webster's Dictionary

For this reason, philosophers rely on the Socratic method, which has been utilized for hundreds of years. The Socratic method allows us to work together to reach the conclusions we need to live a happy life.

> ### THE SOCRATIC METHOD:
> "The method of inquiry and instruction employed by Socrates especially as represented in the dialogues of Plato and consisting of a series of questionings, the object of which is to elicit a clear and consistent expression of something supposed to be implicitly known by all rational beings."
>
> Merriam Webster's Dictionary

Our Personal Philosophy

Philosophy on a more personal level acts as our rulebook, guiding us in life. From our foundational beliefs and the different components within our personal philosophy, we form a life, a world. An internal and external reality.

Our personal philosophy will influence:

- Our perceptions.
- Our experiences.
- Our thoughts.
- Our emotions.
- Our words.
- Our actions.
- How we approach and apply ourselves.
- What our human experience will be like.

Based on our understanding of the bigger picture, and the role we play in that bigger picture and on a more personal level, we manifest how our life will be. This is our internal reality: a world created by what goes on inside of us (thoughts, emotions, perceptions) that is determined by the quality of those things.

The external reality is what we build together. You and me. Our external reality is formed by how we utilize our internal understanding, knowledge, emotions, and thoughts, and translate them into actions, words, and choices. It reflects what kind of world we live in.

We'll address this topic in more depth later, but for the time being, just knowing about the world we share, and the world within you, is enough.

What is Our Personal Philosophy Doing Today?

Our personal philosophy encompasses all the key pieces of fact, truth, and/or reality that we believe in. From this understanding of life and the human experience, we determine everything else.

For example, we create the premise that life must be hard, or that it will be easy based upon our understanding of the human experience—that life is filled with pain or filled with love.

If you approach your life with the foundation that the world is scary and meant to be feared, this foundational belief spreads to each area of your life—home, work, family, love, and even your understanding of yourself. As a result, you will act according to this idea.

When you meet new people, you will ask yourself, "Is this person safe?" "Am I safe?" You might even close yourself off in order to protect yourself. By choosing to build your life based upon the Principles of Fear, you are choosing to believe that if the worse can happen, it will. (Notice that I used the word "choosing.")

The simple dysfunctional "truth" that life is scary spreads, influencing the actions and words you choose. When meeting that new person or experiencing that new situation, fear will influence the outcome, which will in turn influence your everyday, personal human experience.

However, if you have a foundation built upon happiness, love, and healing, meeting that new person becomes a completely different experience. Instead of feeling scared and closed off, you might respond in an excited or even curious way. You might find yourself asking, "Who is this person?" "What kind of relationship or connection might we have?" "What can they share with me about the world that I may not have known before?"

The simple "truth" that you are safe colors all aspects of your life, including your choices about the people, places, and situations you surround yourself with.

Our personal philosophy is what all the other areas of our life are built upon. This influence can be positive, or it can taint our experience of life. Therefore, our personal philosophy is crucial.

For this reason, we're going to challenge our personal philosophy and put it to the test. In this way we'll discover whether our personal philosophy is as healthy and happy as possible.

How We Created Our Current Personal Philosophy

From day one, we've been learning about and responding to the world around us. These observations and interactions have culminated into understanding. We take these pieces of information to form the guidebook we utilize today.

We begin with the simple conclusion that if we cry out as infants, our needs will be met, or they will not be met. Then we build upon that.

We look at the world around us; we listen to the words of our teachers, parents, and fellow students. From those words and explanations, our own observations, and the intuitive leaps and conclusions we make, we build our personal philosophy.

We end up telling ourselves that what we know is equal to our human experience. "This is the way life works," we say. "This is what it takes to be successful." "This is as good as it's going to get."

A rulebook is good. We all need guidance to ease our way through life. We need to be able to make decisions that will keep us safe and choose the path that will lead us to great happiness.

Except that not every foundation will ease our way. Some personal philosophies make life harder than it has to be. As a result, we have inadvertently tainted the human experience, reducing it to the boredom and drudgery that we loath. It is in these situations that we wish to be anything but normal and ordinary.

The Mundane Fallacy

As an avid dreamer, I love the many adventures that can be found in stories. I especially love fantasy. But recently I made a sad realization. In listening to a new song from a fantasy TV show based on a book series, I found that the lyrics revolved around not being an "ordinary girl."

Upon hearing these lyrics, my mind started to turn. This is what led me to discover the Mundane Fallacy—the idea that a normal life equals boredom.

We as human beings love:

- Fantasy
- Superheroes
- Sci-fi
- Video games
- Stars (Movie, music, etc.)

We love the extraordinary, and in this way, we have come to loath the normal. We have been taught what it means to be normal, and due to the extreme revulsion we have for the "normal" life, we have created a scenario where we want to be more than human.

Except we are the ones who have created this problem, and the fallacy around it. Being a human being isn't something to be avoided. Being more than human isn't the answer.

We have created an experience of a life that is boring. Then we made the mistake of thinking that this boredom or hardship is because we were mundane humans. But this just isn't the case.

This idea has nothing to do with you or I being boring. It has everything to do with the fact that we've got the understanding of the human experience all wrong.

Being a human being and having a prosperous life doesn't include hardship and boredom. So, let's keep going, because by the end of this book you'll see what I mean.

When we create a personal philosophy based on the lessons others share and what we experience and observe, we can be left with a personal philosophy that holds us back. As I've mentioned, this type of personal philosophy can lead us to place pain into our life, rather than healing from the pain we encounter in life.

What we are taught and what we hear, see, experience, and conclude about life can create coping mechanisms we employ in order to survive. Especially, when we build our personal philosophy with an inaccurate understanding. People all over the world build their personal philosophy utilizing real wisdom and false wisdom. Except we can do more than just survive—we can thrive.

We can do more than just survive; we can thrive:

Why am I encouraging you to make a change? Another foundational component to healing and updating our personal philosophy is that we can do more in life than just survive.

Here's my evidence: Look at the quality and condition of Earth. Not our neglect of Earth, but the potential of Earth. The potential for relationships and family. The evidence of wonderful relationships that we find in stories, books, in our personal life, and the lives of those around us. The beautiful scenery, wonderous lands to explore, and the glittering stars.

We see the potential for great love, healing, contentment, joy, adventure, and exploration, and this shows us that there is the potential for more than just survival.

Here, we're defining "survival" as: the need to breath in and out, eat, sleep, have shelter, water, and safety. This is survival.

We have the option to do more than just trudge through life, surviving. We can thrive.

This is why we are embarking on this healing journey.

Our current personal philosophy has been built upon the wisdom and false wisdom we have gathered during our lives. I would love to say that there is a single reason why we are taught and hold false wisdom.

I'd like to say that because the answer is simple, the solution is simple. The reality is that many factors have impacted our ability to know ourselves.

- The adults that helped raise us don't know themselves, so they couldn't teach us how to discover ourselves.
- Our society has gotten lost.
- Our priorities are skewed. Math, reading, and writing are all important skills to have. But what about our emotions and peace of mind?
- Our pace. If we're busy running around, we don't have time to get in touch with ourselves. We can end up running away.

- We grow. We change. Knowing ourselves is a constant process of **practice**. (You'll find I love this word.)
- The coping mechanisms that kept us alive and safe in childhood don't support us as adults. They stop working, but we keep using them until we learn to replace them.
- We have lost our connection to Spirit, and as such lost our history. History impacts us on many levels.
- We don't even know what the human experience is anymore.

There are many reasons as to why we are currently living with a personal philosophy that holds us back. What makes this reality even sadder is that we have not been taught or even told that we can question these pieces of wisdom. Whether we receive information from our superiors, the adults in our life, or what we have been exposed to, we must learn to question it, to put it to the test.

When we only utilize what we have been exposed to, we are left with a portion of reality, because what we experience is only a small piece of the big picture. When we keep our current philosophy without putting it to the test, we are left stuck, stagnant, and trapped.

This is what facilitates boredom. Growth, evolution, and healing will never happen. A greater understanding of the human experience won't be achieved. Greater moments in our lives will not happen. Love will not be experienced.

So put your personal philosophy to the test.

Healing Our Personal Philosophy

When we heal our personal philosophy, we heal ourselves on every level. While ending a dysfunctional habit is wonderful and leaving a toxic relationship is momentous and both are deserving of celebration, these are examples of small healing.

The reason you entered that toxic relationship is still there. Maybe it's a piece of false wisdom in your personal philosophy—that lie taken as truth that tells you what you deserve in life. Like what people think is more important than what brings you joy.

Or maybe it's a past experience that you took as fact. Like when you had a challenging teacher and then you came to believe that school and learning is hard. These components in your personal philosophy endure, even if the relationship or habit is healed.

In choosing to heal our personal philosophy, we are choosing to make changes on every level. That self-doubt you have that influences all your relationships is healed. That belief that life is torture is healed.

In this way we don't just heal a symptom of the false wisdom, we heal the source, ending the chronic pain we endure. We take life to the next level. We do more than just survive; we begin to thrive.

For example, when I was little I built my personal philosophy based on what I knew and what I thought I knew. Then as I lived my life, this roadmap guided my way. Providing me with answers and guidance, and because of this I was led astray on my journey.

Like anyone with dysfunction and false wisdom in their personal philosophy, we can end up taking detours and being led down dangerous and hazardous roads in our lives.

Even when you change the visual or top layer of your dysfunction, deep at the heart of things, you might still be taking the journey with a faulty map. It's like placing a band-aid over a broken heart.

It wasn't until I took the time to stop and take a look at what I was thinking and doing, that I began to unearth the heart of my pain. In doing so I started my healing journey.

When we desire true healing, we need to go straight to the source and analyze what makes up our personal philosophy. You are a soul living as a human being, and that means something. It's influencing what you know, how you experience life, and how you understand reality—all the components of a human experience.

We need to analyze our personal philosophy, so we know what world we live in. Do you live in a world where you know yourself? Is it a place where you will poke yourself in the eye every day, or is it a place where you place your hand over your heart? Your personal philosophy sends a ripple effect throughout your life and the lives of others.

Therefore, we need to take the time to question our personal philosophy. What it is we think we know. Hold it up the light and turn it so we can see all sides. Tip it upside down and give it a shake.

Although it will take us some time to go through these steps, when we're done with the process, what we will be left with is a personal philosophy that allows for growth and promotes healing and happiness. We will then combine our understanding of the human experience (that bedrock) with a principle (how we will approach our life).

After we have that foundational piece in place, moving forward will become so much easier, and more deeply aligned with life's possibilities. We'll have broadened our mind, increased our opportunities for happiness, and increased our understanding of how our world works. We'll know how we work within this world, and we'll know how to balance all the components that create a thriving human experience.

Rather than being overwhelmed, keep reading. We are taking this journey together, you and I.

Analyzing Your Personal Philosophy

The prospect of analyzing your personal philosophy can be daunting. When I made the realization that something needed to be done, I took a long journey with many twists and turns. When you go about winging it, the journey can leave you feeling absolutely depressed and lost.

But in winging it, I discovered tools that worked, and ones that didn't. I also discovered in what order to approach this journey. As a result, I did what I needed to do to be successful for myself. I also learned what I needed to learn in order to share this process with you. (As was the plan all along, although I didn't know it at the time.)

In putting everything I knew to the test, not only did I rediscover what it means to have a human experience on my terms, but I also took a similar journey as one of my teachers, Descartes.

Descartes was born in 1596, and he started his journey by taking his personal philosophy and hitting the delete button. He acknowledged that he knew nothing about life or reality, and he thought for a long time, until he had the epiphany that he was real. He thought, therefore he existed.

From this foundational piece of information, he set about rebuilding his personal philosophy. In my own ignorant way, I did the exact same thing ten years ago. However, I started with the question, "What is my favorite color?"

When I knew that I had lost myself, I had the realization that I could take nothing for granted. Since my separation from the core of myself happened subtly, I couldn't know what was me, and what was the influence of my dysfunction. I couldn't even know if my favorite color was accurate.

From that simple thought, I spent my time rebuilding who I was and what I knew about myself from the ground up. Taking the time to think about what I liked, what I didn't, what I believed and valued, and what my inner truth was. Without knowing it, I was building a new personal philosophy.

This is exactly what we are going to do, except we are going to use the knowledge and wisdom of others to aid in our journey. In this way, your healing journey can become easier, without all the doubts and worries about what you're doing and how it's all going to work out.

Analogy of a Basket of Apples

René Descartes utilized the analogy of a basket filled with apples in *Meditations on First Philosophy*, to describe the process he went through, and I want to share it with you. Each apple represents a piece or component of your personal philosophy, except some of the apples are rotten (false wisdom & dysfunction).

Descartes posed this scenario and then pointed out the problem. How do you go about picking out the rotten apples to save the wonderful gems within your basket? Just as rotten apples will infect the healthy apples around it, so will dysfunction.

Descartes' solution is to dump out the basket and inspect each apple, one by one, then return only the healthy apples to the basket. In this way you can preserve the wonderful wisdom you have gained in your life and still purge all that is harming you.

I want to utilize Descartes' analogy because it is very clear and concise. My recommendation is to dump all of your preconceived notions about life, all the apples of your personal philosophy, onto the ground, and work with me as we inspect each apple and return only the healthy ones to our basket.

The truth is that we all have dysfunction, we all have false wisdom, and this false wisdom will continue to be passed down from generation to generation unless we dump out our basket and remove that false wisdom now.

A lot of healing and a lot of improving our life is actually looking to our past and unlearning the false wisdom and dysfunction that we have acquired through our own misconceptions and through the misconceptions others have shared with us, or even forcibly thrust upon us.

So, we will dump out our basket and inspect each apple. Putting what we think we know to the test.

Putting Your Personal Philosophy and Others to the Test

When we create our personal philosophy, we build it upon foundation beliefs (our bedrock). In putting our beliefs to the test, we must be willing to give them up in order to achieve the changes we need to realize our dream of a better life.

> ### FOUNDATION BELIEFS:
> "The core beliefs that we build our perceptions about life on."

Be prepared to test and question every single piece of your personal philosophy, my personal philosophy, and the personal philosophies of others. You'll want to do this for two main reasons.

First, if you automatically assume that a piece of your foundational philosophy is healthy, you might miss something. You might overlook a spot on an apple when you place it back into your basket that down the road will stand between you and your dreams.

Secondly, what I need and what you need are two different things. We both need love, healing, and acceptance, but on a more personal level, my life looks different than yours. As well as where I am in my life.

We have experienced different things and exist in different environments, with different careers, family members, ideas of success, goals, and desires. These differences impact what you need from a personal philosophy in order to support your individual and special life.

In this book, I am going to share my personal philosophy, my understanding of the human experience, with you. I have spent years working on it, and at its core, there lies an understanding to life. But the intricacies and quirks of any personal philosophy are just that: personal.

For this reason, I want you to question my personal philosophy. I want you to put my personal philosophy to the test. Don't just ask whether I am right or wrong—ask if this is what you need; what you want.

Because this is your personal philosophy. You have a greater chance of love, healing, and happiness when you tailor your personal philosophy to the quirks and intricacies of your individual and special self.

Take what works for you and leave the rest. I am not obligating you; I am not pressuring you; I am not putting you in a position where you must accept every single foundational belief that I am about to share.

The foundational components that we'll cover in the next section act as the framework to a healthy and healing personal philosophy. They are the bedrock of a human experience. From there I will add additional components that make up a human experience based upon the Heart-Centered Principle. (For example, choosing to approach your life from a place of love rather than fear.)

As you begin this journey you might start off with one or two components, and as a time goes by, you might build onto your foundation, or renovate it, and that is wise and extremely healthy.

Because our life will change, and you will grow. In order to reflect that change and growth, we need to reevaluate how we approach life, so that it reflects who we are today. In this way our foundation remains relevant to our current human experience.

Due to these reasons, we are going to become **belief contingent**, always remaining open to something greater, something grander. To truths, facts, and realizations we have not held before. If you find some holes or gaps in my personal philosophy, it is because I don't yet have an answer to those areas.

So instead of putting a bad apple in my basket, I am going to leave that space open for something I can't even imagine. Something that could be the most wonderful thing I have ever learned or been shown.

A lot of your personal philosophy will be influenced by how much you know, by getting that data. By talking to people and discovering the different perspectives that each of us have. This can be extremely beneficial in our own understanding of what we believe and know to be true.

The Three-Part-Test:

To test the wisdom you possess and will encounter, follow these three philosophical steps.

Step One: Understand

When you encounter an apple of your personal philosophy, when you read about mine, or when you encounter somebody else's beliefs, **ask questions**.

Do what you can to learn all you need to in order to better understand any given belief or piece of wisdom. What are the arguments or pieces of evidence that make this information real wisdom rather than false wisdom?

Step Two: Challenge It

The second step is to challenge this conclusion or "wisdom." Do the arguments work? Can they be challenged? Is the argument correct but the conclusion wrong?

Calling something wisdom is not enough, you need to be able to hold it up to the light, turn it around, and shake it while it's upside down. That way no hidden blemishes make their way into your basket.

Step Three: Decide

After you understand and have challenged this apple, decide. Is this piece of wisdom real or false? Does this information help you in your life? Do you need this foundational belief? Do you completely agree, or do you need to modify the conclusion or argument? What do you think about this apple? **Will you be throwing this apple away, or placing it into your basket?**

With these three steps you can analyze and test each apple you encounter. In this way you can pick out the pieces of wisdom you want as a part of your personal philosophy, and decide which ones are best left on the ground.

Needing Faith with Your Personal Philosophy

In the world of academia, the focus revolves around learning the facts, finding the right answers as opposed to the wrong ones, learning the dates, learning the techniques, and meeting the requirements for the degree. But philosophy is a dialectic, a conversation. It's about putting everything you know through the wringer.

This is where things get shaken up. We are putting all the things you have taken for granted to the test, and while your foundation is being tested, you are up in the air.

A lot of people don't know what to do when this happens. Shaken and uncomfortable are sensations we generally avoid, unless we're experiencing them in a controlled setting (like, a movie theater or rollercoaster ride). Therefore, we are going to do more than create our personal philosophy.

Philosophy as an academic focus is about conclusions and arguments. Nothing is true, real, or guaranteed in reality without arguments and evidence. If we only operated within the confines of this academic purview, we would be without large chunks of our personal philosophy, waiting for the evidence and arguments to show up and make those parts real.

Because of this, I've discovered that we need more on a personal level. We need faith.

I don't just mean faith with regards to a religion, but a faith in things we have not yet proved or have an answer to—faith in apples that we are pretty sure are real, but that we have not yet verified by philosophical standards.

Academic philosophers disregard faith. For them, faith is worthless. But we are not just philosophers; we are human beings.

The Three-Part-Test: Philosophy and Faith

I want to take this topic and apply the Three-Part-Test. This will help you understand my reasoning about needing faith.

Conclusion

We first start with a "conclusion," or piece of wisdom (an apple).

Philosophy requires that we can know, explain, understand, and argue everything in reality that we can deem real and true, Descartes' example being, "I think therefore I am." This means that we as human beings are able to understand and know all things about reality.

Arguments

After a piece of wisdom is shared, there are pieces of data, facts, and/or evidence that prove this wisdom is real rather than false. We call these pieces of evidence "arguments."

This conclusion is predicated upon what we are capable of understanding. Based upon this assumption, anything we can understand and argue is real. But it's built upon the assumption that we can understand all things, that we are capable of understanding all the information and truths about reality, life, and our place in it. In this way, we can uncover the truth of life and the human experience.

The Three-Part-Test

After we have been exposed to this apple, we put it to the test. This will help us to determine whether it's real wisdom or false wisdom, and if we need it in our basket.

Step One

Understand it.

I understand this belief/conclusion that "We are capable of understanding all things that are real and true. Thus, we have no need for faith."

Step Two

Put it to the test. Here are the thoughts I had about this belief.

The human brain is amazing. It is capable of so many different things. It has an elasticity, with a natural inclination to snap back. For example, our body always has this natural inclination to heal and to be in a healed state.

But for all our brain's capacity I look at history, even today, and at some of the new things being discovered.

From this I have reached the conclusion that our brains do not possess the knowledge to understand everything. We can understand our lives, but that doesn't make us rocket scientists, biologists, or mathematicians. Our brain is only capable of so much.

Step Three

Decide what to do with this apple.

In philosophy, if you can only count on the things you can understand, you leave out a lot of different areas and topics that we as human beings need to incorporate into our foundation. Because of this, we also need faith.

Our faith will act as that bridge between what we know and what we hope is true, or what we feel deep within us is true. That bridge between philosophy (what we can understand, know, and can argue), and those other areas of our lives. That leap of faith, as it were.

As a philosopher, not having faith is ok. But we are not just philosophers. We as human beings need more to function and thrive within the environment of this world.

Which means that I will not be accepting the apple that says we can know and understand everything about reality. In my opinion, that apple is best left on the ground. Instead I will be placing the apple of faith into my basket.

I not only made this decision based on arguments but also due to personal experiences. Having been raised within the metaphysical community, I witnessed from a young age, things that defied "logical" understanding. But nevertheless, they happened and were real. This taught me that there is more to this world than one might initially believe.

When we analyze what we think we know, we not only utilize the arguments but our personal experiences as well. Sometimes we have seen or lived through something that will provide a stronger piece of evidence than any argument.

As you've just read, this is how we go about testing and healing our personal philosophy. We encounter apples, put them through the test, and then decide what to do with them. What did you do with these two apples?

Just like we did with philosophy's belief about faith, put what I share to the test. Understand what I'm sharing and critique it. And don't just critique my philosophy—critique yours. This is **your** personal philosophy.

This has nothing to do with what another person feels, thinks, or decides how we should feel or think.

It is ours. It is personal. The purpose of our personal faith is to guide us—you, me. Not another person.

Why it's Ok to Test Your Faith and Your Personal Philosophy.

Faith is a delicate subject for a lot of people. I know that when I call upon some people to critique their faith, the apple they currently have in their basket, they might feel like they're treating their faith dishonorably. This is because that for many people their faith includes a god or goddess.

My viewpoint is this: there is no dishonor in questioning, critiquing, or striving to have a greater understanding of your faith. When we choose to put our faith to the test, we get more deeply involved.

Our faith is no longer just something that collects dust on a shelf. It is something that we pick up and inspect; something that we spend time with and connect with.

For myself, I believe Spirit would have a greater appreciation of how I treat my faith when I choose to test it rather than leaving it on the shelf to gather dust. Therefore, we need to critique what we believe in.

When we consider the amount of knowledge that our brains can comprehend, we can see that we are always learning. We are always in a position where we can stretch ourselves and learn more. In this way we fill our basket with apples and construct a safer and happier roadmap for ourselves.

It is when we become static that we stop living. In those moments we are merely existing. To live means stretching ourselves to try new things. It means taking on new thoughts and ideas, seeing how they work, and if we want to keep them. Living means more than just being successful.

Success is wonderful, feels wonderful, and is a wonderful experience, but if we never fail, if we never learn something new and enter that awkward period where we're uncomfortable, are we truly living? Are we stretching ourselves and broadening our mind? Are we opening ourselves up to a greater reality than we know? Are we connecting with those around us?

Speaking for myself, my faith has key components that I have inspected and chosen to place in my basket. But there are a lot of open holes, and while open holes might be a trigger for worry or concern, I look at it this way: my gaps in understanding demonstrate the respect and honor that I have for my faith.

I don't have all the answers. I don't have a complete comprehension of creation, our purpose here, or the role we play on a grand scale—not just on this Earth, but within our Solar System. I leave room for that. I acknowledge I just don't know.

That way, when I come across a new piece of information, I can inspect the apple, put it to the test, and decide whether or not to place it in my basket.

My argument, in philosophical terms, is that testing your faith is not dishonorable treatment, but instead a way to solidify and strengthen it, to broaden and build upon it. We are making sure that we are not being led astray by the false wisdom that is sometimes created by the misunderstanding by ourselves, others, and spiritual leaders.

I call upon you not to be afraid of questioning these pieces of information. In this way you will be left with the raw, true form of faith. You will emerge bigger, grander, and open to more. You will have connected with the truth of things. You will be living.

> ### POTENTIAL ROTTEN APPLE ALERT:
>
> I also encourage you to think about why you would feel that questioning your faith is dishonorable. Or if you were affronted by my suggestion, why you felt that way. Was the way you felt built upon your personal philosophy that you are not to question your faith? Was it built upon a foundation of fear, shame, guilt, or panic?
>
> If it didn't come from your perception influencing how you heard my challenge to question your faith, are you requiring external validation for what you believe? Do you require somebody else to tell you that you are right to believe in your faith?
>
> If I disagree with you, are you able to say, that's ok, this is my faith? Or are you going to want to fight me or prove me wrong in order to prove yourself right?
>
> Are you holding onto a rotten apple that is bringing pain and worry into your life?

Your personal philosophy needs to be built upon internal, not external, validation. Not only is your personal philosophy and personal faith, well, personal, but people in the world around you are not in a place to determine what you need from your personal faith.

Their influence might not be for the better, and that might be accidental or intentional. There are people out there who intentionally attempt to cause harm and pain. So, when you compare or discuss your personal philosophy with another person, understand that it is not their role to tell you whether or not you are right or wrong.

You might learn something from their perspective or from their understanding of your personal philosophy. But ultimately, they have no guaranteed power or influence over you or your personal philosophy. Any power they seem to have is power you choose to relinquish to them.

The same can be said for your faith. While there are many people who may share a similar faith, whether they are Christian, Buddhist, Jewish, Muslim, Hindu, Taoist, Wicca, etc., ultimately, it is your personal relationship with Spirit, your personal faith, that matters most.

Be careful when you choose which pieces of information to place into your basket. Each time you choose to place an apple in your basket, critique it and evaluate it. When you place it in your basket, do so with the knowledge that it is a healthy apple. That you are placing a stone within your foundation, as opposed to dumping all the apples in your basket willy-nilly. That you, in that moment, are helping to create a human experience that you'll love and thoroughly enjoy.

When you choose your faith or your personal philosophy, search all around you for new apples. When you challenge and test what you know and think, you open yourself up to a world of possibility. There will be times when you forgo an old apple for something new. There will be other times when you discover that an apple you already have has given you the safety and happiness you desire, more than any other piece of wisdom you have found.

Faith is choosing your ideas, morals, and beliefs out of everything else you know. If you only know "A," that's all you'll believe. But if you know "A-Z" and still choose "A," you demonstrate a healthier and stronger faith.

How it Feels to Heal Your Personal Philosophy

In choosing to heal our personal philosophy, we are acknowledging that we are in pain. That our life is less than we thought it could be. We are putting our beliefs to the test. We are re-evaluating what we know, taking all our understanding about life and how we fit into the world, and turning it upside down and shaking it. All so we can achieve a thriving life.

Yet it is through this healing process, that we have the potential to throw the world on its head. I'm speaking from personal experience here. For myself, I discovered that everything you have naturally assumed, everything that has cushioned you throughout your whole life, will not be there anymore.

During times of self-growth, I would step back and rely on my safety net. That is until I realized that it was my safety net that I was healing and re-shaping.

Normally when we heal, it's from a relationship, habit, or situation. We fall back on our roadmap, utilizing the wisdom we have collected in life to guide us as we move forward. But in this instance, it's our personal philosophy that we're healing. Doing so will bring about a new sensation and new experience.

In the process you might notice just how many areas and instances in which your personal philosophy has influenced or directed you. When this happens, take the opportunity to look at this influence and realize how important your personal philosophy is. Gather your own data. Let that realization sustain you through this bumpy portion of your healing journey.

As with all healing, there are wonderful moments and there are painful ones. We are addressing dysfunction and wounds. To purge false wisdom means implementing a change.

While we might be seeking to get rid of our pain, it not only requires a knowledge on how to do so, but also a willingness to release the things that have brought us pain in the past. There are going to moments when you won't feel comfortable. This is ok. It is natural and it is nothing to feel bad about. You'll be feeling icky in a different way as it is. There is no good that comes from piling on an extra helping of uncomfortable.

Because you have released thought patterns that are no longer helpful or good for you and implemented new ones, you may not yet be comfortable with what you have put in place.

We are not just pack animals; we have created an environment where we get comfortable with our current settings. Thus, we are often creatures of habit.

As a result, change, whether it's changing our perspective or our actual environment, can be uncomfortable. We like what we're used to, we like what we know—sometimes to the detriment of our mental, physical, emotional, and spiritual well-being.

In those instances, I encourage you to look at what has triggered this change. Look at what has stimulated your drive and desire to live a different life, to embark on this journey of healing with me.

Maybe it was an experience or trauma, or maybe it was the realization that your life was harder than somebody else's. You want to live a life that is happy; you want to be surrounded by love, fulfilled, and successful. You want a thriving human experience, and for this reason we are turning things onto their heads in order to make them right and healthy.

LETTERS TO SELF:

There are two letters that I would like you to write to yourself.

The First: A Positive Letter

I. Write this letter when you feel great or have a connection with the world and Spirit. Tell yourself how it feels. How happy you are. How you are feeling with this new way of life.

II. Mail the letter or keep the letter somewhere safe.

III. Read the letter when it gets back to you or pull the letter out when you feel threatened with backsliding, when you're doubting this new path, or when you are at risk of falling into old thought patterns and habits that no longer serve you.

The Second: A Negative Letter

I. Write this letter on the worst day. Tell yourself how horrible you feel and how you wish life would change. Share all the things that are propelling you onto this journey of self-discovery, self-care, and self-love.

II. Mail this letter (let the universe send it back to you when it's meant to) or keep this letter.

III. Read the letter when you get it back or drag it out when you forget what the past was like, when you are thinking of going back. Remind yourself that there is a reason you wanted a change.

Example: An Apple Put to the Test

We've discussed personal philosophies in the form of apples. This abstract analogy has helped me to teach you what we're going to do. But abstract formats can leave me feeling somewhat confused on the practical application side. So, what I've done is provided an important piece of wisdom that I then put through the Three-Part-Test. Take a look.

My Conclusion

Learning and life is an act of building.

Step One: Understand my Arguments

Argument One

Sometimes a dysfunctional piece is what we need because it fills a part of our life. A piece of dysfunction can remain because it's not time to change yet, or because we need to address other areas of our life before we work on it. Sometimes we need to learn a new apple that will then replace our dysfunction. It might be a multi-step process.

When I started to dig deep into my dysfunction I found evidence of this multi-step process. I put my co-dependency, relationships, perceptions and in this case, my word choice, through a multi-step process that help me get them to a loving and healed state.

Regarding my word choice, I first focused on *"should," "could," "would," "have to,"* and *"must."* The idea of "should" denotes stupidity. When most people say it, it's a derogatory statement that communicates they're stupid for not knowing the answer. *"Have to"* relinquishes our power.

As I continued with my life, I began to eradicate my excessive use of these phrases. In doing so, I changed my way of thinking and understanding. Moments where I had at one time felt powerless, became empowering for me. I discovered a new truth, that my personal human experience can be anything I desire. How I saw a situation changed, and thus, how I lived changed. All along, it was my understanding that dictated whether a situation was a powerless or powerful one. Not the situation itself.

At the time, they were great words because I needed them to communicate. But as time progressed, and as my healing has progressed, I needed to rebuild how I communicated.

I then took things to the next level and am now working with the word and idea of "*make*." I am building upon older healing in communication and taking things to the next level.

You can bring things into my life and expose me to things that might influence me to be happier or sadder. But it is still my choice in how I respond to that situation. I was using this word, "*make*" all the time, and for the time being it was good. I needed a word to use.

But after I learned that first piece of knowledge, I started to build upon it. To expand my moments of self-empowerment. Now "make" is a word that I rarely use. I make cookies. But I do not make people happy. I work to bring happiness into my life and when other people share in my life and share in my environment, there's joy in that environment, and they can choose to be a part of it, or they can choose to have a pity party.

Argument Two

I like to use the example of reading because it shows us that knowledge is an act of building, that there are certain components that we need to have in place before we move on to the next step.

Before we could read novels, we needed to learn each letter, their individual sounds, and what the combination of letters create.

Then we started to sound out words. C-a-t, cat, m-a-t, mat. Through that process, we built words, then we built phrases, then sentences, which became paragraphs and chapters, which became books. From there we built our vocabulary. C-a-t, category.

It's just like in every other aspect of our lives. Before you become an energy healer, you need to know about energy. If you don't even know energy exists, you're not going to become an energy healer.

The same is true with the healing of a wound, a life, or a foundation. The healing of one wound will lead you to another. As a result, you'll heal deeper and deeper, achieving a more peaceful state.

My point is that it's not a one and done. You don't learn c-a-t and then you're off to a novel and life is good. You're building upon your knowledge. You don't heal a hugely co-dependent relationship and be done; you might notice teeny tiny co-dependent habits in various relationships that still need healing.

It's coming back, digging deeper, going layer by layer, because as you heal the dysfunction of this lifetime you might come across dysfunction to heal from a past lifetime (which we'll cover later). Or maybe you go through stages.

You might experience great hatred and over time you slowly process and heal. Each time we come back to a wound, the hatred turns to anger, to sadness, to acceptance, and then peace. As life progresses, you'll build on what you know, creating a more prosperous human experience.

Step Two: Critique It

Does my conclusion make sense? Do my arguments make sense? Which do you agree with? Which do you disagree with?

Step Three: Decide

With this new knowledge, what components aid you in your personal philosophy? Which did you choose to help you build a strong foundation, a caring lifestyle, etc.?

Here's Another Example

Conclusion

Bullies don't operate on healthy wisdom. As such, in order to live a healthy life, we won't take on their false wisdom as truth.

Argument One

When I was a child and encountered rude people, my mother would ask me one question: "Do happy people act that way?"

With this single, simple question, she helped me create a healthy perspective for what I had just witnessed or endured. Because of this, when I encountered my first bully (unfortunately not my last), and she called me "stupid," I didn't take on this piece of false wisdom about myself.

When a person tells us something, or treats us in a certain way, they are communicating to us. They are telling us what they think about us. But like anything, when we encounter a new apple, we **need** to put it to the test.

What authority does this bully have? None, really—because we know that happy people don't act that way. If this bully isn't happy, then they don't have an accurate understanding of the human experience. They are living their own life with false wisdom—false wisdom they are attempting to share with you as they remain stuck in survival mode.

So, now that we know this person has no authority or logic to the things they say and do, what will you do with the apple they are trying to force onto you? Will you keep it or leave it dropped on the ground?

Argument Two

In my learning, I have come across many people who taught me that we are only capable of sharing what we know. Think about it: can you teach microbiology if you've never learned it? When you apply this knowledge to people who choose to be bullies, rude, harmful, and hateful, you discover something interesting.

You discover that how people treat others is based on what they know. Which means that people treat you the way they treat themselves. How sad is that? When a bully yells or physically harms you, it's because it's what they've witnessed, experienced, and built their personal philosophy on. They are not only berating themselves within their mind and maybe even physically, but they are berating the world around them.

When you consider the harm a bully does, think about that harm being used against themselves. Is that the kind of life you wish to live?

If it's not, then do you really want to learn and believe what the bully has told you? Are they in a position to share wisdom with you that matches your human experience built upon love, healing, and happiness?

The Three-Part-Test

Step One: Understand It
Does it make sense that we can choose to not listen to what bullies have to say about us?

Step Two: Critique It
Do my arguments make sense?

Step Three: Decide
What will you do with this apple on how to respond to a bully?

What To Do as You Heal Your Personal Philosophy

The thing about approaching your personal philosophy in this manner is that it requires time. It takes time to dump out all your apples out onto the ground and inspect them one by one before placing the healthy ones back into your basket.

I began my healing journey the summer before high school, and it took years to put what I knew to the test. Not only that, but to try out and learn what tools and pieces of wisdom would help me on my journey.

Some of the apples you inspect won't be healthy. They will be dysfunctional or contain pieces of false wisdom that will no longer, or have never, benefited you. They will sometimes need to be replaced.

The only way we can replace them is by striving to learn more. For example, if you are in a co-dependent relationship, you do not possess the knowledge on how to live a healthy relationship until you are exposed to those pieces of knowledge.

Sometimes you're going to bump along and learn these new pieces of information and sometimes you'll need to seek them out. You need to seek them out for your benefit, because you love yourself. You began to love yourself with your first breath.

Start learning today. Right now. Let me share with you the information you need to create a healing, loving, and happy human experience. All you need do is turn the page.

Take Away Part One:

- We each have a personal philosophy.
- Our personal philosophy is created by what we know, are taught, see, and believe.
- Our personal philosophy is filled with wisdom (apples) and false wisdom (rotten apples).
- Our personal philosophy determines the quality and condition of our lives.
- Due to this, we must test our personal philosophy.
- The Three-Part-Test:
    - Step One- Understand.
    - Step Two- Question.
    - Step Three- Decide.

PART 2

My Personal Philosophy

I hold my dreams
deep within my soul
intangible to the unknown

eternal flameof
light & darkness
turned shadow

turned to shadow
within the abyss of night
transformed am I:
    a preservation for my own

my own being
Proud & Stubborn
holding its own

born from the conjuring
of man & women
yet I am not

not man nor women
I am ancient

struck into existence
before the kindling of Earth's core

not defined by body,
but by my soul

I am

I didn't start with, "do I even exist?" as Descartes did. Instead, I started with, "What is my favorite color?" When you realize that you've lost your way or even lost yourself, your first thought revolves around what to do. How do you rediscover that healing and happy path in life?

The second realization you'll have is that you can't take anything for granted. It's all up in the air and it can feel like you are building yourself and your life all over again. The journey is new and foreign.

But we are never the same as when we were first born. What we have experienced up until this moment has shaped and influenced us. We carry those memories and lessons. Rather than attempting to return to the past, the healthy approach to healing and happiness is to move forward. Into a future that we create based upon our dreams and desires.

This book is here because I have this belief, this faith, that life can be better. By you reading this book, I'm thinking that you share that same idea, that same hope—that there is more to life than what we currently know. With this belief, I traveled a journey that was filled with many unknowns.

From not knowing my first step, to not knowing where I was headed, most of my journey was clouded in shadows. With only the moon to light my way, it took several years before I would come to understand what my journey had accomplished.

The knowledge I set out to acquire was meant to answer the question of "What do I do now?" How do I re-discover myself and live the life I desire? As a result, I read everything I could get my hands on, and tried different techniques and tools. Absorbing all the information that might provide me with an answer.

PART 2: MY PERSONAL PHILOSOPHY

From this knowledge I have improved my life, and I am now going to break down the bedrock of my personal philosophy for you. I am going to share what it means to be a human being and how it works.

Our personal philosophy starts with the bedrock of the human experience. From there we add tools and principles (like love) until we have that personalized roadmap and guidebook for our dream life.

In sharing the foundational beliefs of my personal philosophy, you'll get to see the conclusion and argument system in action. This time, you'll be the one to put these conclusions and arguments to the test and decide for yourself just what it is you believe.

While the foundational beliefs and various components of my personal philosophy can act as your foundation, the details are up to you. You might not agree with everything that I believe in. My arguments, conclusions, and perceived truths might not all resonate with you.

As I've said before, while I am sharing with you the foundational components to a healthy personal philosophy, you are not required to take anything you don't believe in.

This is still your personal philosophy. While we will work together, it is still your choice which apples you choose to adopt and which you choose to leave.

Let's get started...

Conclusions and Arguments

My personally philosophy is built upon a few key components or foundational beliefs. From those foundational beliefs, we create an understanding of the human experience.

> **FOUNDATIONAL BELIEF:**
> "The core beliefs that we build our perceptions about life on."

These Ten Conclusions weave together, building a human experience. As I cover each conclusion about life and reality and offer my arguments, they will build onto one another to create a human life.

Conclusion One

I started with the same conclusion that Descartes uncovered. "I think therefore I am." I believe and I have built my foundation upon the conclusion that I exist. That I live, here and now.

Argument

I reached this conclusion utilizing Descartes argument. "I think, therefore I am."

Conclusion Two

The second component to life is that you exist.

Argument

Right now, all I know for sure is that I exist. But, if you were merely a figment of my mind, my imagination, you would be living the life I wanted you to. The world would look and be exactly how I wished it to be.

Except that people don't always do what I wish they would. If life was what I wanted, we wouldn't have wars or violence. No one would be in pain.

So, if life doesn't match my desires, then you must exist. You are doing what you wish and desire. Then it is through our decisions that we co-create and co-exist.

Conclusion Three

Currently, all I know is that you and I exist. But for all I know we could be floating bubbles of thoughts. So, with our next conclusion, we will create the world.

Argument

While Descartes found the external world's existence as unreliable, I dove into other philosopher's points of view and found those who believe in the existence of this world. When we have no control over people and things in the external world, the world must exist.

Since we don't always get what we want, we aren't in control of others, so they too must exist, as we saw with Conclusion Two. If they exist, we both need a place to exist. We can then prove that the world we live in exists, because we each see the same thing.

When I look in the mirror, I see what you do, and what the camera sees, too. When I look out my window, I see trees and mountains, the stars and moon, and you see these things, too.

This lets us know that the world exists and isn't just a figment of our imagination. If it was a figment of our imagination, some people would be living with dinosaurs and others with unicorns.

From these arguments, as well as this deep feeling of truth I have within me (faith), I know that I exist, as well as you and that which is around us.

Conclusion Four

Conclusion Three is that this Solar System exists and because it exists, we need to address how it came into existence. I believe in a creator who molded this Universe, Solar System, and our planet into existence from raw energy.

Argument

The reason I believe this to be the case is that in order to create a planet where we can sustain life there are many minute factors that needed to be exact and precise. In order to have a world where human bodies can exist, we need a specific kind of environment.

The distance from the sun is a factor. Too close, we'd be too hot; too far, we'd freeze to death. We needed to be at a distance where we are just warm enough and just cool enough where we can thrive.

Then, when you factor in the composition of the Earth, having an atmosphere that allows us to breathe, oxygen and water, nutrients, etc.— different factors that require such precision according to mathematics and science—it is of my philosophical conclusion that we are not a fluke accident. We are an intentional creation. And intentional creations come from a creator.

From these conclusions and corresponding arguments, we know we exist and know that we are an intentional creation, whether our creation was through seven days, a big bang, an evolutionary factor, or a combination of them all. No matter how we came into existence, our existence came through an intention, by a creator who from this point forward I will call Spirit.

Now, you might be thinking that we're working with some pretty big picture topics here, but keep following along with me, because all of these conclusions about the reality of life are building upon each other to cover what it means to be a human being and have a human experience.

This knowledge is essential on our journey, because once we cover these foundational pieces, we can apply them to our own lives. In addition, we can weave in our Heart-Centered Principle to create a unique human experience with a focus on and goal of love, healing, and happiness.

But these steps can't be addressed until we have the basics of what it means to be human. Our bedrock.

Conclusion Five

The next step is to look at our creator, Spirit. Knowing we have a creator wasn't enough for me. I wanted to know more about the nature of Spirit, so I looked around me, at all Spirit has created, down at my own body, and I looked at those I call family. As a result, I came to the wonderful conclusion that Spirit, our creator, is loving and kind.

Argument

Spirit has created a planet that holds such great beauty, healing herbs, and rejuvenating water and food, to name just a few. As such, I know this place isn't where we just exist or even survive, but a place where we can flourish. (Whether we thrive or not comes down to other factors.)

Because of this argument, my conclusion is that we have a loving Spirit. Now, this Spirit might be a God or Goddess, but that will require another set of arguments.

For myself, I define Spirit as:

SPIRIT:

"The entity or sentient being that took raw energy and formed the Universe, Solar System, Earth, and our souls. Weaving together a complex existence."

> ### PHILOSOPHERS POINT OF VIEW ON GOD:
> When philosophers reference God, 99.9% of the time they are referencing the God of Christian faith, Christ. They define their God as an omni god (all-powerful, all-knowing). So, if you choose to study philosophy in order to strengthen your personal philosophy, keep in mind that that is the God who philosophers refer to.
>
> Whereas, when I reference Spirit, I am not defining Spirit as anything more than the sentient being who manifested with kind and loving intention all known existence.

Taking the conclusion and arguments of our existence, an intentional creation, we were able to build upon them and discover more about our human experience. Specifically, we discovered that we have a loving creator.

These three components are what we're going to build the rest of our understanding (our rulebook) on. These components shape everything else that I believe in and every other point of philosophical conclusion that creates a complete look at a human experience.

The Three-Part-Test

We're not done yet, but I want to take a moment and have you stop and consider what you've read so far.

- Do you understand my conclusions and arguments?
- Do you agree with them or are there some errors?
- What will you take with you moving forward? (Which apples will you place into your basket?)

The three main components are:

- We exist. (Me, you, & the Solar System.)
- We were intentionally created by Spirit.
- Spirit is a loving creator.

As you can see, we can build upon our understanding. Just as we uncovered the type of Spirit we have (loving), we have more to uncover. So, let's go deeper.

When we have a kind and loving Spirit, what does this mean? When you take this fact, we discover that Spirit is going to do all Spirit can, to love us, guide us, protect us, and nurture us.

Then when you apply the knowledge that Spirit is a loving and supportive creator, we get to learn more about the world we live in, ourselves, and the potential our human experience has.

Conclusion Six

We have a soul.

Argument

This conclusion was hard for me because I not only have faith in my soul, but a knowing. As I mentioned when we took a look at philosophy and faith, sometimes our life experiences are stronger than the arguments themselves.

In this case, my knowledge that we have a soul predates any conscious consideration. Due to my past life memories that I have been experiencing since I was a little girl, I have known that we have souls for years.

With past life memories, I have not only come to believe in reincarnation (which we'll address soon), but that we have souls as well. Because while the body dies, I continue. I am a soul in human form.

But I also know for others, without past life memories, that this argument is not enough. As a result, I went in search for answers. I investigated philosophers and what they had to argue.

What I found were long articles and complex arguments, based on the conclusion that we, each of us, have a soul. But this wasn't enough for me, so what I did was fall back on my personal philosophy (my safety net and roadmap.)

I called on my spirit guides (whom we will also address later) and asked them for help. In response, they shared with me this argument to support the conclusion that we have souls.

My spirit guides drew my eye to the world around me. To my inner thoughts and logical mind, and what I discovered was that you can't explain all of life with just a body.

A soul is needed as a foundational belief for us to comprehend many aspects of life. Such as…

- People: There are those with whom we have deep connections. People who, on a faith level, we know we've known before.

This would be reincarnation. We can only attain this through something that doesn't die when our body does, something that can carry on and experience life again. That something is a soul.

- Miracles: There are times in our lives or the lives of those around us when recovery/experience/intuition happens. If we are only a human body and all we are is relegated to our brain, these things wouldn't be possible.

Conclusion Seven

As souls we have all of eternity.

Argument

I cannot fathom a Spirit where we are destroyed without very, very good reason. And I have not found a very, very good reason as to why we would be destroyed after a single lifetime. After all the hard work that went into creating us and in having a loving creator, it would be cruel to end our existence.

So, we exist in the moment we are created with kind intention, until the end of existence. That's a long time to exist.

> ### ARGUMENT (FOR OUR SOUL)
>
> When we are created and have all of existence, we can look at history and know that there has been life before we were born into our current bodies and we know that there will be more to life after our bodies die. So, how can we exist for all of existence if our bodies die? We can only do so if we have a soul that lives separate from a human form.
>
> This idea strengthens my faith that we have souls.

Conclusion Eight

From this perspective, when we are created with intention, purpose, and focus, we are here for a reason.

Argument

A child that is asked to sit quietly in a corner for the rest of their lives is going to be bored. And if you consider it, this scenario fills the criteria for abuse and negligence in most countries.

When we're talking about a loving Spirit, I don't envision Spirit as abusive. When we are gifted with all of eternity, we are going to be gifted with the opportunity to learn, grow, experience, and to thrive. In this way, we can honor our existence and purpose.

Conclusion Nine

One of the ways we are going to be given this opportunity is to be student and teacher, in a safe environment, like a school. This is how I define us here on Earth. We are born into human bodies to learn, teach, and experience; to spend our existence not stuck in a corner but growing.

When we grow, we have growing pains. Not all of what we learn will be easy or fun, but we are in a safe environment, an entire planet to learn upon. Not only that, but we are supported, and some of this support comes from the family we have, the teachers and community.

Argument

We exist now in bodies. When you consider this reality, you can see that there is a reason why we are here. Rather than sitting in a corner for all of existence, we get to live. To experience. To delight in life.

As you view life from the perspective of a loving creator, life becomes a community and not a competition. Rather than being left to fend for ourselves, Spirit supports us, and we support each other.

As a result, we end up creating an environment where we have support while we learn and grow. We support those around us, just as Spirit supports us, and those around us support us.

Currently, most people aren't consciously aware of this mutual support. So, the community we have exists beneath the surface, but it also has the potential to become a conscious part of our lives. This is where we begin to understand and know that we are a community on a deeper soul level.

The Three-Part-Test

With this next layer to what the human experience means, how are you feeling? Has your understanding of life changed at all? Do you agree with me or disagree? How do you feel about my understanding of the universe?

When you take that simple conclusion that we have a loving Spirit, you can apply that information to your perception and to every aspect of life. Taking these foundational beliefs, how can you reanalyze your life? How can you utilize this new knowledge to update and heal your perceptions?

Conclusion Ten

Because we are intentional, loved, supported, guided, and because we have all of eternity, we are not being forced to learn, grow, and experience life on a short timetable. We are not having a test placed before us and told that we have twenty minutes to ace it, or we're doomed.

Because we are not being mistreated, we have a lot of opportunities. We will experience forgiveness and compassion, and one of the ways we will experience this is through reincarnation.

Argument

We are here to learn, experience, teach, and grow. But this cannot all be accomplished in a single lifetime. In addition, not every single lesson and experience can be had in a single lifetime.

For Example

Consider the life you were born into. The people you know as family, the environment you were raised in. Consider your education, gender, culture, society, what you've done with your life so far, and where you envision yourself going.

With these considerations in mind, can you see how your life is limited from all its possibilities and has been narrowed down into a single lifetime? What kind of family did you not experience because of the one you had? (Loving vs hurtful, rich vs. poor, rural vs metropolitan, etc.)

You are only able to experience a certain amount in each lifetime. In order to experience it all and learn all you can from each situation, you need many lifetimes.

For this reason, and through all the effort Spirt went through to transmute raw energy to create life, an entire Solar System, a planet and all the intricacies within this one planet, we are going to be here again.

Not as punishment, but as an opportunity. The truth is that we don't need to learn it all by the end of our lifetime. It is not a fail-or-succeed situation.

It is very much like a Montessori school setting. The student drives the learning, and we determine whether the student was successful or not based on their participation and effort.

When you look at life in this way, with these key components to your perception, you remove a lot of potential for fear and hardship. Not only do I hope for and believe in a happier world, but I believe a happier, healthier, and loving world is the reality.

With our Ten Conclusions, or bedrock, in place, we are starting to enter into a strange new reality. While these are foundational beliefs you may already have, they might not be ones you've deeply considered. Whether you're new to these beliefs or they're old friends, there comes a moment for all of us to take that leap of faith.

When I was starting out on my healing journey, I thought about everything. Sometimes I thought until my head hurt, all in an attempt to find answers to all the questions floating within my mind. While I have a lot of answers now, I still think a lot.

As I sat down to put into words what my healing journey had taught me, I thought a lot about how to explain life to you. How did I take my personal experiences and put them into a format that would make sense?

Through contemplation, meditation, and research I came across the philosophical style of conclusion and argument. In this way I can share what I know to be true without needing to say, "Just believe me…I know what I'm talking about."

But in the end, logic and reason is not enough. We do not possess the skill to step back from our human experience and comprehend all things. Which means, that the evidence for some of the things we are talking about (like souls and reincarnation) is missing.

There are some things that fail to meet philosophical standards. While you may choose to wait, until the argument (the logic or evidence) manifests, this is also the moment where you may choose to take that informed leap of faith.

What do you know to be true, deep within you? Just as love cannot be measured in a glass beaker, some things defy human comprehension.

The Special Truth

With the Ten Conclusions above, we have built an understanding to life and the human experience. Yet, it is rather broad. Our next step is to look at you. To learn of the special truth about you. So, take a look at this conclusion and my argument.

Conclusion

We are each of us, important and special.

Argument

What I bring to the table is a puzzle piece to life, and the reason it is a piece of the puzzle is that we are all interwoven. We are all supplied a piece of creation. Not only in information, perspective and understanding so that we may aid and broaden the minds of others and connect with one another, but because life as we know it would not be the same without each and every one of us.

It might be easy to see that with a president or spiritual leader, but the same can be said for every single human being.

For Example

Let's look at one person. By having one conversation with you, they may show you a world that you have never seen before or provide you with a piece of information that you have never thought of before.

In this way, we impact the world around us. This one conversation will impact you and how you see and interact with the world moving forward. This impact would never have transpired had this person not been here.

If I were to provide you information about a wheel, give you this round object, your life would be changed. We might never meet again, but in providing you with this simple little thing, you will never be the same.

You might create a car or a cart, changing the way you travel or move things. In any event, this little thing will impact your life. Not only your life, but you may share this information with someone else. Or they might see you living your life with this wheel and as a result, a hundred years down the road we will have motorcycles, bikes, cars, and a way of life that we did not have before.

A single person, a person we did not even know, had this ripple effect. Each of us have this power. A power to not only change our own lives, but the quality and condition of the world.

This ripple effect can be enacted by something someone says. Even if we don't understand or remember it right away. Twenty years down the line, we might recall their statement and it may trigger something within us, helping to aid us.

Without that one person planting that seed, our lives might be radically different. This shows us that each person is important. That the world we live in today is due to every single one of us being here and our ancestors before us.

If you took one person out of the equation, we wouldn't know the ramifications. We wouldn't know the outcome. We would be living a different life, and because of this—because it wasn't just one person standing up against tyranny, but hundreds; it wasn't just one person voting, but hundreds—our life, our reality, our collective, has become what it is today.

This simple fact could be perceived as incomprehensible, but it shows us that we are important. We each play a vital role in life and whether that vital role has a detrimental effect or a positive one is determined by us.

In taking responsibility for our lives, we can come into our power and positively impact the world around us. While this concept might be overwhelming when viewed through a perception and life philosophy built on fear, it goes to show us how precious we each are. Life becomes a gift when we see it through the eyes of love.

Whether you knew this before or not does not change the fact that for every single day that you have lived, you have been having an impact on people and the collective. So, rather than choosing fear or panic, we can choose joy through this one simple fact, where we find that we all matter and are important.

Yes, we could flee; run away and remove ourselves. But even when we remove ourselves, we are going to influence the external world. That effect is probably not going to be positive, because as long as you are here on Earth you have a chance to improve life. It might not be a huge, monumental thing, but it might be exactly what someone else needs. And since we are each special, if you help just one person, this is a wonderous thing. Because that one person is special, too.

For that reason, we all carry with us a piece of the puzzle, a piece of the collective. I might not know the name of the person who invented the wheel, but they matter to me today.

You matter to me. You matter to life, to all of us.

The Three-Part-Test

Having shared the Ten Conclusions and Special Truth that are the bedrock to the human experience, I have opened my internal world to you. You are beginning to understand the world based upon my perceptions—how my eyes see life.

It is in this way that we begin to build our life—from these core foundational beliefs into a wonderful world, a loving creator, and the gentle reality of our personal life, our thriving human experience. Every other aspect of my life is impacted and influenced by what I have just shared with you. It represents my understanding of the human experience.

From this point onwards, you will build on the foundational beliefs that craft a human experience. I have chosen to build onto this foundation with love, or more specifically a Heart-Centered Principle. With principles, we decide how we will approach and live our human experience.

In combining the Heart-Centered Principle with my personality, I have ended up creating a personal philosophy filled with quirks. A personal philosophy that doesn't hold me down or fight with me, but one that supports and honors who I am.

You will do the same moving forward, starting with your understanding of the human experience.

Which conclusions did you choose to add to your basket? Which apples got left on the ground? Did you need to modify them?

Next, I want to walk you through my understanding of reality, of how the world works according to the human experience I have just shared with you. But before we get into that I want to share another fallacy I have discovered in my pursuit for that thriving human experience.

The Fallacy of Assumed Knowledge

While reading about my foundational beliefs and just how to go about analyzing your own personal philosophy, have you felt ignorant or stupid? Has there been a moment where you felt that the knowledge I have shared with you is knowledge you **should** have already possessed?

As a child we know that we don't know much. So, we ask questions. We say, "Why?" "How come?" all the time. We end up bugging the adults in our lives with our un-ending curiosity for the world around us.

But as we start to grow up, we lose our way. We start to know things, and somehow, we make up the false wisdom (rotten apple) that we are supposed to naturally know answers to things that we have had no exposure to. We assume that certain topics are obvious, or that we already know the answers. Of course, as the joke goes, when we assume, we make an ass out of u and me.

As I was working to discover my personal philosophy, I kept running into moments of depression and feeling stupid because I didn't have the answers. That is, until I discovered the rotten apple at the core of my problem. It was the idea, the *assumption*, that I was supposed to already know everything.

We, as a society, have been taught and end up teaching this rotten apple to those around us. Until we are all left feeling stupid; when we aren't. We assume knowledge all the time. We assume…

- That people know how life works.
- That people know how to be polite, communicate, and be in healthy relationships.
- That people know how to be intimate.
- That people know how to work and be responsible or have fun.

- That people know how to do everything that human beings do, even if they've never been exposed to those things before.

Whether it's knowing how to build your personal philosophy, knowing how to communicate, or knowing how to be in a healthy relationship (whether it be with friends, with our jobs, or with romantic partners), this knowledge, while assumed, is not downloaded into our brains at birth. These are skills we all need to learn.

Some people can learn these skills by looking around them or by winging it. Sometimes we need to check out a book from the library and learn. Ask questions. Become a child again. There is so much knowledge out there for us, that the truth is you will never run out of "Why?" and "How come?" questions.

Rather than assuming that you should know this, take a different apple with you. Approach these scenarios with the knowledge that you don't know, yet, and that's ok. Choose to be gentle and loving towards yourself, (and to those around you) just as Spirit is with you.

Now that we've got that rotten apple out of our way, it's time for me to apply my personal philosophy to life. To the human experience.

Take Away Part Two:

- Ten Conclusions create the bedrock of a human life.
- The Special Truth- is that we are each of us important and special.
- As a direct result of this Special Truth, we can see evidence of the power we have in life. Not only to create a thriving human experience for ourselves, but also to impact the quality of life here on Earth for all.

PART 2: MY PERSONAL PHILOSOPHY

The Ten Conclusions

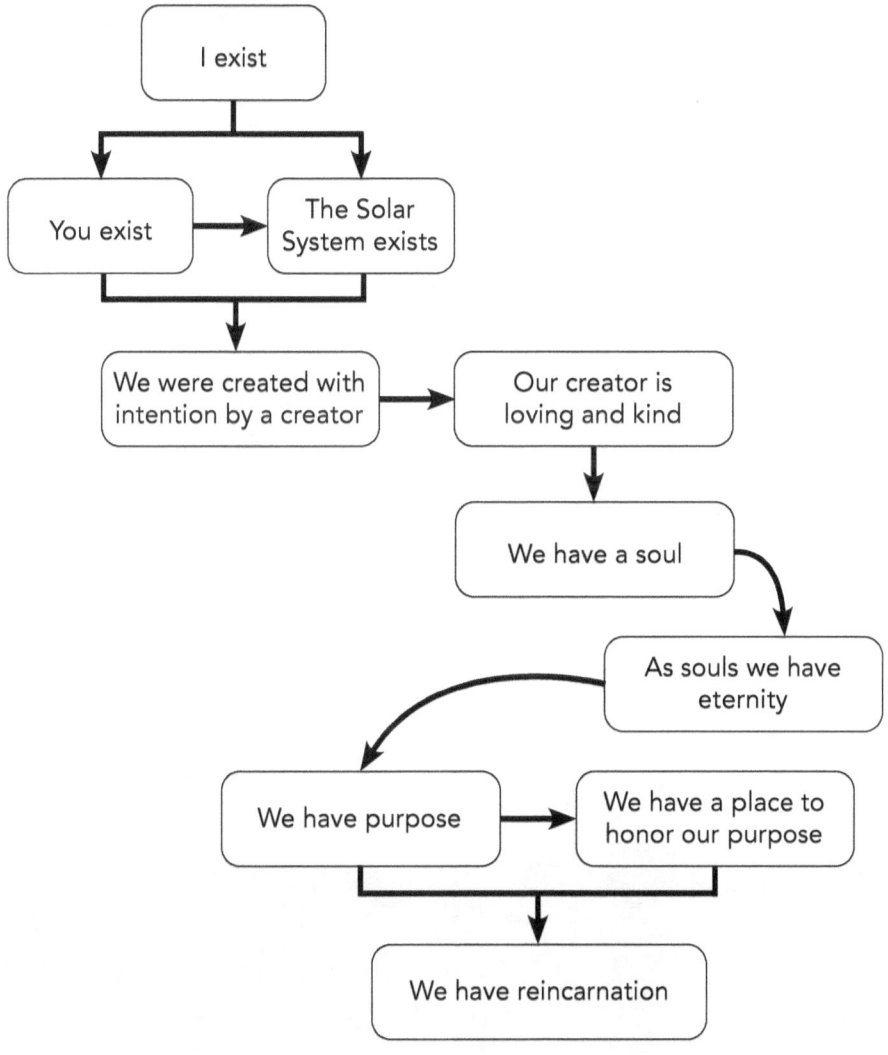

PART 3

The Human Experience – Life as I Understand It

long ago I found
    my path to be my own
my rules, my desires, my passions
stood apart

and since my way was new
I journeyed & studied
seeking my truth

the way I live is me
the way I see & breath

I stand deeply rooted
I may sway & bend
but I have yet to break

break from what I know to be
the way for me

As a human being, I have strived to understand life and just how I fit in. In building my personal philosophy, I have been pulled between being a soul and being a human being. I have been pulled between the physical world and the spiritual one I have come to remember. This internal tug-of-war left me confused.

The tension between these two sides of existence threatened to tear me in two. Until I sat with my understanding of life, and answers began to form.

I am a human being. I am a soul. These two seemingly disparate forces are not at odds with one another. When I thought about the big picture, I discovered that the knowledge and answers I was seeking, revolved around what I needed today.

In having this epiphany, I came to understand that all answers about my life came down to the human experience I am currently having. I am a soul in a human body. My happiness and prosperity in life revolves around this lifetime. In focusing on learning about the components of my human experience, I learned what I needed to thrive today.

In the first part of this book, I introduced you to the unseen force that is our personal philosophy (our understanding of life). I then shared with you the foundational beliefs that create the bedrock of the human experience. Now, let's take that information and apply it to our personal lives.

From this information, I'm going to break down how a human life works. In this way we'll keep building to our end goal—a personalized human experience where we thrive.

The Steps of a Single Human Experience

Step One – We decide to be human beings

When we consider a loving Spirit, we learn that we are here by choice. We wanted to come to Earth and be human beings. In this environment we can learn, teach, grow, and accomplish all manner of things. As souls, our curiosity, dreams, and desires have led us here.

In having chosen to come to Earth, we are going to be cared for as we always have been. Now as I mentioned, we choose this lifetime, but when we address the concept of destiny and free will, there is a lot of debate. Do we make our own choices? Are we puppets, or are we real?

This is what I know to be true…

That with a loving Spirit, we are guided. This guidance starts with our creation and continues each moment we exist, including before we start a lifetime.

I equate this guidance we experience to a meeting with a school counselor. Before we enter college, we have the opportunity to meet with a student counselor. This meeting centers around what we want to learn.

In this meeting, the questions we answer and the information we share informs our counselor about who we are and what we dream. From this information, our counselor can aid us in shaping our college experience (a personalized human experience).

- What do we want to learn?
- What do we want to experience?
- Who do we want to meet and connect with?
- And more

In basing our decisions on our character and desires, we build a plan for college. Our plan is shaped by our desires, the wishes of others we know (fellow souls), and what we can do for the collective.

If you equate this analogy of school to life, we know that we are going to meet with Spirit, our spirit guides, and even fellow souls (fellow students) before we are born.

We are going to be asked, "What do you want to learn?" "What do you want to experience?" "What is the personal journey you want to take?" And how do you want to intertwine with the world?

From this information, we are going to build an itinerary for the journey of our life. This itinerary is called a Soul Contract.

SOUL CONTRACT

"The plan, roadmap, or itinerary that we create as souls with the aid of Spirit, our spirit guides, and other souls, shaped to guide us during the lifetime we will incarnate into."

With all of life's limitless possibilities, we narrow down what we will or won't experience, whittling the great expanse of human life into a wide and wonderous journey—a single broad lifetime condensed for our understanding and enjoyment.

This itinerary gets crafted with the full knowledge of our soul and the wisdom of Spirit. This is how we choose a specific human experience. From this plan, we are going to be given guidance and support in seen and unseen ways as we live our life.

PART 3: THE HUMAN EXPERIENCE – LIFE AS I UNDERSTAND IT

Step Two – We are born

Our memory of that meeting might be washed away, but it is still something we have set up for ourselves. Because we have chosen lessons and experiences for ourselves, and even other souls we want to meet and interact with, we have components of our lives pre-planned: our destiny.

> ### DESTINY IS
> "our free-will choices made before birth."

Then we have the idea of free will. We have these moments planned in our lives, and the presence of free-will "is how we are going to perceive and experience those moments."

For Example

We might choose the lesson of self-love. As a result, that might mean that we learn to love ourselves no matter what the external world tells us.

We could be born with the destiny of being a social outcast:

- Either through gender identification,
- Sexual identification,
- Ethnicity,
- Or social class

Through the experiences common to these circumstances, we will experience external hatred. This opportunity provides a human experience/lesson where we can learn how to love ourselves no matter what anybody else chooses to say, and no matter what the external world chooses to thrust upon us.

It's Got To Be About Faith

One of the most challenging moments for us is when we experience, or witness someone we love experience a torturous or traumatic moment. It is in these moments where our mind rebels against our foundational beliefs.

With war, injustice, and extreme violence how can this be a wonderful world? How could we possibly be protected and guided? How are we safe?

In my own life, I have encountered such moments when my mind rebels against the truth I hold within me. It is in these moments that I am presented an opportunity to learn and to grow. To remember that we are souls and human beings.

Just as we saw with philosophy's perception on faith, there are times when the human mind doesn't know. There are some things in this world that defy human comprehension.

We don't know the exact specifications of our destiny, the destiny of those we love, not even the destiny of the world. These unknowns play a major role in the "whys" and "how comes."

It is within these moments as we endure or witness unacceptable behavior, that faith is required. Faith can be simple in theory and easy most days, but it is when the logical mind rebels against the truths we have come to know, that we truly experience faith all on its own.

I find a peace and strength with my foundational beliefs when I combine two key factors. The first is that we have a loving Spirit, who does all Spirit can to comfort us and guide us. The second, that we have free will.

As individuals and on a collective level, we make choices that support or challenge Spirit's wonderful world. Yet despite all the stubbornness we sometimes exhibit, we are still loved. Spirit still supports and guides us.

As a result, you are not the only ones on a healing journey. We as a planet are on one too, and like any healing journey there are painful and wonderful moments. Moments that build upon one another to lead us to a world and life of prosperity.

We have a choice, and this is our free will coming into play. Our free will determines how we are going to learn this lesson—if we are going to struggle against it, fight it, and make it harder than it needs to be, or if we are going to embrace the lesson and learn it quickly and safely. This is our present day free-will. It dictates how we respond or react to an experience or lesson.

Step Three – The Soul & The Solar System

As we have uncovered with our Ten Conclusions about the human experience, we are souls in a human body.

Our understanding of the human experience is built upon these ten foundational beliefs. But our human experience comes from us: soul and the world we live in: solar system.

The quality and condition of our journey is influenced not only by our personal philosophy, but by the balancing of soul and the solar system—in essence, our internal and external realities. We briefly touched on this aspect of life before, and now I'm going to dig deep into this component of the human experience.

Your Internal Reality – Soul

In life, we go about learning and experiencing everything. We live a human life and based on the decisions we made before we came, the decisions we've made in the past, and what we decide today, we shape what kind of human experience we will have. We decide if it will be based on fear apples or faith apples.

Our internal reality comes down to our soul and our human body. Comprised of all our inner thoughts, emotions, perceptions, and personal philosophy, this part of our world remains in our control.

While this inner world does not include the outer world or people around us, it leaves us with this awe-inspiring power. The power to create any kind of life we dream of. It is in this area that we have been focusing and will continue to focus on.

For Example

There are times in our life when our preparedness and our chance for happiness will be dependent on our present-day free will. Did we pay attention in class or not? Did we actively participate in our lives or merely act out our role?

In choosing to reach deep into our power and claim responsibility for our lives we discover that our life is our way. We see evidence of this truth when we look at how we have chosen to live our life. These choices determine the quality of the ripples we send out. So, when that test or lesson comes, how smoothly it goes becomes dependent upon how we respond in the moment and how well we prepared for it (whether unknowingly or knowingly) in the past.

PART 3: THE HUMAN EXPERIENCE – LIFE AS I UNDERSTAND IT

My preparation to write this book began years ago. From the college courses I took to my own journey in discovering my personal philosophy, I have not only been enjoying my life, but I've been laying the building blocks to an even bigger and brighter future.

I didn't know I would write a book years ago. As I mentioned, when I was on my healing journey, I didn't know it was leading me here. But by paying attention in class, taking the classes that appealed to me, and following my intuition, I was acquiring all the building materials I needed to succeed.

As a soul, with the support of Spirit and my spirit guides, I set up my life (Soul Contract) to thrive. How well this plan works comes down to my present-day free-will. How easily this book gets written depends on how prepared I am.

This is how we are meant to live our lives. We took the time to build our Soul Contract; it is now time to have faith in it. To know that as we live our life, we will have addressed each component of the human experience:

- What we desire to experience, learn, teach, etc.
- What we've been asked to assist in.
    - This could be a fellow soul asking for our help, or something for the Universe.

Our itinerary is set; the quality of our journey is determined today—right here and now, as you utilize the power of your free-will to decide the condition of your life.

Your Life, Your Way: Responsibility

In the beginning I talked about how we create our own personal philosophy starting on the first day we're born. With each cry and each wiggle, we observed the reaction from the world around us. Each action and, in time, each word we chose—the ripple we sent out into the world—elicited a response. In this way, we learned about life and added this data to our personal philosophy. This shaped the understanding we have of our human experience.

The choices we've made demonstrate to us that our life has always been in our own hands. Our internal reality lies within our control, and can only be influenced by the outside world. That's the power we have—our life has always been in alignment with our way. How well we've utilized our power is another matter.

As we shape and create the human experience we desire, we must become accountable for our life. In doing so, we do not change anything that wasn't always true. The responsibility has always been there. The only difference is that we are now consciously embracing the ability to determine the quality.

This is that power I didn't know we had. The ability to choose a different path. One that will lead us to adventure and happiness and away from pain and anger. Once we willingly accept the power we have in our own lives, we must have the perseverance and persistence to do something about it.

Here is where we learn that the healing journey you have embarked upon with me is real and true. In having responsibility for your life, you hold the power to make changes. To heal and transform your life into one of prosperity.

Consider This

When your hand comes out for a handshake, what raises your hand?
– You.
When your arms come out for a hug, what raises your arms?
– You.

It would be easy to blame your life on others. To not be responsible for your reality and the impact your reality has had on the people, animals, and places around you. But this would not make it true—the life you're living today is a direct result of the choices, words, and actions that you have taken. While this truth can leave us feeling overwhelmed, it doesn't need to.

Accountability: this one basic idea has the power to reshape your life. We stop waiting for others to wake up to our needs and desires and then do something about them, (which is not their responsibility.) We end up taking accountability for the reality of our life, not only for the abuse and destruction, but the ability to make changes and reshape your life into one of happiness.

When we have rotten apples in our life:

- We settle for "good enough."
- We perpetuate unhappiness, dysfunction, and negativity in our life and the world.
- We block ourselves from opportunities, hopes, and dreams.
- We can become depressed, ill, and even aggressive.

- We scare away those who are happy and healthy. (They have taken responsibility for their lives and don't want to be around the rotten apples in your life.)
- In short, nothing good.

With responsibility you can use a self-hate apple and beat yourself up over the mistakes and neglect. Or you can dump that apple onto the ground and pick up a new one. An apple of self-love.

Choosing to beat yourself up for past mistakes that impacted the condition of your internal reality and life in a negative way won't help you. It will only act as a block to future and even present-day prosperity.

You also don't help the world by prolonging pain. But by embracing healing and self-love, you also introduce it to the world. You send out a ripple that, based on how you use the power of your responsibility, has the potential to do great good.

Our External Reality: The Solar System.

When we realize that we are not alone, that we are connected with one another, we also acquire the knowledge that we are supported and guided. We understand that we are united, and this unity means that the wars and healing we enact out on Earth will influence not only our personal lives but the lives we are connected to.

If we were to gaze upon the Earth from the Solar System we could start to draw parallels and apply a new understanding to life. While our personal lives are the only things in our complete control, we also have an influence on the world around us. I want to take this time to address the connection we share.

As we just saw, our internal reality is your perception on life, built by your personal philosophy and how you utilize your free-will. While our external reality is comprised of all other components of life, from the people, animals, to the places, and experiences.

So, if I've just shown you that your internal reality is what it's all about, why does the external reality matter?

Argument One

What another person says or does has the capacity to influence your internal reality. This argument is going to aid in the conclusion that the external world matters.

When a person says to you, "I love you," or says the opposite, this act has the potential to influence your life. It has this potential for a couple of reasons.

- If you have an unhealthy apple in your basket, you might be in a co-dependent relationship where you give another person power to dictate your life. Until you remove that apple and reclaim your power, the external world, that person, will have more control over your life than you do.
- Another way that the external world can influence our internal reality is through the information that we gather. Our personal philosophy and our perceptions will be built upon, tweaked, and refashioned to reflect what we have learned and experienced. This is a part of how we learn, and it is our experience of human life that comes from the external world.

What you're reading here is from the external world, but it is having an influence on your life. It is showing you a different way to look at the world. It might be something that you read and share, or something that you read and forget about. As a result, your life will change in a small way or huge way. The external world is influencing you.

That doesn't mean that we are giving up our power. It merely means that we are considering a new perception or piece of information, a new apple, brought to us by the external world.

Argument Two

My second argument is that you play a role in somebody else's life. It might be on a personal level, such as with family or friends. Or your influence might be on a larger scale.

How you treat your friends and family, influences the quality of their lives. Even voting, boycotting, or utilizing your money and purchases to speak for your beliefs has a large impact on the world. You are influencing others on a small scale and on a grand scale.

When you approach another person and say, "I love you," or the opposite, your words have the potential to influence that other person. You have become the external world to another person.

Argument Three

While Earth acts as a personal classroom for us, with our own personal environment, (family, lessons, experiences, or situations). We also have a global family. A global experience. You play a role in that global family. Without you, life would be different for a number of reasons. Remember that Special Truth?

The external world that we live our life in has come into creation by Spirit. But the current state of that creation is dependent upon and influenced by you and me. By all of us.

Interconnected Reality: Soul & Solar System

In order to achieve an understanding of the link between our soul and the Solar System, we need to look at the various components that create our reality. Our life.

Society is merely the collective perception on life; a rule book or a way in which we measure success, or what we perceive to be a good life.

In America, history teaches us Manifest Destiny. This is the idea that we are God's gift, or that we have a right to be here and do whatever we please, all in an effort to pursue our needs and desires.

But what Manifest Destiny excludes and precludes, thus violating the true nature of things, is that we are all interwoven. There is an interlocking component or ecosystem to life that we all share. And this fact about life is going to impact whether our personal philosophy is accurate or not.

In your personal life you are not a solitary being. We are pack animals; we are interconnected. What I do will not only impact my internal reality, but it will impact yours and those you share a house with, a town, a state, a country, and a globe with.

What I do here and now will have a ripple effect, and with all these ripples that we each make, we as a collective create the world we know.

> ### LIFE IS LIMITLESS: A NEW APPLE
>
> I want to take this opportunity to share with you another building block you can add to your personal philosophy. When we create our personal philosophy, we build on what we already have.
>
> For example, in combining the two truths—that we have a loving Spirit and that we are all interconnected—we can learn more about the world and life.
>
> When we take the potential we have here, that was given to us by a loving Spirit, and add the powerful influence we share over the quality of life, we learn that life is limitless.
>
> Earth has the potential to be a thriving paradise thanks to Spirit, and we have the power to make it that way.

Step Four – Living Life Today

In leading a healthy life there is a balance that we must practice finding—a balance between our internal reality and the connection we have with the external world. This unity can be tricky to discover.

In choosing a healthy lifestyle, we are choosing to practice a balance between soul and Solar System, and this balance is what can drive us nuts, especially when we are in a perfectionist mood.

Because this balance shifts from moment to moment. We are currently in a world that is attempting to pull us into a million pieces. We are being asked to exist in the past—not only in our own life, but in the lives of past of generations.

PART 3: THE HUMAN EXPERIENCE – LIFE AS I UNDERSTAND IT

We may have to deal with resentment carried by alienated cultures, genders, races, and ethnicities. Or familial wounds. Due to the inheritance of these wounds, we are fragmented in the past.

Then we are being fragmented into the future. These are the goals you are forever striving towards. Once we have graduated the next goal is a career, family, legacy, and beyond.

Littered in our personal and global philosophies are apples that are rotten, and even healthy ones that, due to the changes of Earth, have become rotten over time.

Society and functioning on Earth requires some thought for the future to be a successful one. Yet, this can be achieved without pulling ourselves apart.

Right now, we are being fragmented into the future, fragmented into the past, and our current life is being fragmented into home life and work life. It's wounding us, and I just don't accept that.

We can find balance, we can say, "enough, no more!" and we can choose not to let the preexisting world dictate our fragmentation. We can weave ourselves back together. We can learn to achieve that balance rather than being ripped a part.

The human experience is the weaving together and balancing of each force in our lives. It is when we do this that we not only live a human experience, but a thriving one.

In simpler terms, we achieve a thriving life by approaching each moment of our life with wisdom. That in this moment you are currently living, and the ones to follow, you pull together the different factors of living, you carry information about life, and apply this wisdom to how you live. Not only does this create a thriving moment (healthy apples- understanding/relationships/choices/actions) but helps to perpetuate this state creating a series of thriving moments, which are what make a thriving life.

These various factors are...

Factor One:

We are going to look at our personal philosophy because it will determine how we experience life. If we end up taking that path of pain or one of adventure and happiness. Then we pull in principles as we decide how we will live our lives; with fear or healing and love.

This was the focus of my healing journey during high school. As I traveled from classroom to classroom, and completed the necessary assignments, I spent my free time absorbed with finding the truth to life.

In asking those big questions, putting things to the test, and thinking about what resonated with me I was building a personal philosophy. Not only through the knowledge my teachers had to share with me but through my own research and observations.

Factor Two:

We are going to look at what we have planned for our life. Not only will this clue us into the big picture that is our life, but it will also address our responsibilities for the Solar System (Soul Contract).

Following high school, I started to test my thoughts and ideas with real world application. As I went to college and experienced the adult world, I gathered data on my new knowledge and beliefs.

Yet it wasn't until I was asked to take a huge leap of faith, that I stopped testing my truths and started living them. In having completed my AA degree, obtained my TEFL certification, I got a job in Honduras to teach English.

PART 3: THE HUMAN EXPERIENCE – LIFE AS I UNDERSTAND IT

With a plane ticket all set and a contract in hand, I went to my healer proud and excited. That is, until she informed me that this was not my path. That the life I was meant to lead was right here, a path beyond my sight because it was beyond my realm of knowledge.

What would you do? Would you cancel this job opportunity, stay and trust in the itinerary of your life? Or would you take the job and follow society's idea of success?

Well, I canceled that plane ticket, apologized to the school principal, and stayed. It was at this time, that I took what I knew about myself and what I believed and put it into action.

My old worries about what others thought creeped back in, and it provided me with another opportunity for a deeper level of healing. All while I began to truly live my life based on the truths I had spent years discovering.

The process while at times frustrating and hard, helped me to solidify my inner truth. To reclaim the power I have over my internal reality. To change paths once more. This time, to a path of healing, love, and happiness.

Since my healing journey began and my leap of faith, my life has drastically changed. Not because a revolution happened, but because I see with new eyes and feel with a stronger and wiser heart.

Factor Three:

We're going to look at who we are as people, because that will influence our life and will also influence the external reality. We will decide who we want to be and make choices that reflect this desire.

The work I have done not only addressed the human experience but me personally. Remember, I lost myself. While learning the truth of life helps me live a wonderful life and working in tandem with my Soul Contract helps me achieve my dreams, it is through self-discovery that we develop that personalized human experience.

In re-discovering who I am and who I want to be as a person (what my influence on the external world looks like), I am able to uncover concrete answers to what brings me joy. What my desired human experience looks like.

Factor Four:

We will address the wounds, dysfunction, and bad apples we have from this lifetime and the ones before. In this way, not only will we reap the benefits of healing and improve our human experience, but we will also help the world to heal.

My journey started because I discovered that I cared what others thought about me, more than how I felt. While this realization is what triggered my healing journey, I have also worked through various ideas and beliefs (rotten apples) that have limited my life in other ways.

This healing continues to this day, as my healing reaches deeper into my internal world and as my life expands. As I live, I enter into new situations and experiences, that unearth new and old beliefs held by me or by society. With each rotten apple I release from my personal philosophy, the greater my life becomes.

Factor Five:

We will add knowledge and tools to our personal philosophy, creating our own unique guidance in life. So, as we live life, we do so with support, love, and guidance.

As that high schooler, we are asked what we're going to do with our life. We are faced with options for classes and careers, that will help us shape our lives. But even deeper than that, is how we will approach our life.

If we will be fearful, closing ourselves off from life. Or if we will embrace the community we share with love. (That Heart-Centered Principle.) In this way, experiencing excitement and merriment with the new people and experiences that are headed our way.

Factor Six:

We will never stop growing. From old tools to new wisdom, when we keep our minds open, we improve our life with each encounter and experience we embrace.

With ten years of healing under my belt, you might be thinking that I've got it all figured out. That I've spent enough time thinking about life, myself, and where I'm headed.

The truth is, I haven't run out of questions. In choosing to actively live my life, to embrace my human experience there is always something new to try, read, or witness.

This is the marvel of the world. When we stop looking to the past or the future yet to come, we are greeted with a wonderous sight. With a zillion paths to choose, where each one will take us on a new adventure.

The truth is, with ten years under my belt, I'm just getting started.

With these factors, we are going to pull all this information into the current moment. When we apply what we know each day of our lives, we set ourselves up for a thriving human experience because life is happening right now. This second.

Application

With all you've read, I want to address what's going on today, because you might not be living that thriving human experience yet. All these steps on your healing journey are wonderful, but we are inspecting those apples one-by-one. And while that is the only way we can be truly successful, it takes time. Yet there is no reason why we can't start enjoying our lives now. Right this second.

Life Happens in The Present Moment: A New Apple

The truth is that we are meant to live in the moment and cherish life, but through false wisdom we have ended up creating a life where we have neglected our desires and our health in favor of things yet to come.

Conclusion

For most of us, we don't know what we have in our soul contract. We don't know when we said, "uh I think I'll be done by this point," or "I want to try this…" We have this moment,

PART 3: THE HUMAN EXPERIENCE – LIFE AS I UNDERSTAND IT

and the present moment is where we live our lives. As a result, the present moment is what's important to a thriving human experience.

Argument One

The present moment is all we have for sure. The past is just that, the past. It's moved on, even if we haven't. We can anticipate the future, and it is smart to anticipate it, so that we can not only function but thrive in a world where there is society, deadlines, and various obligations. Yet, the present is all we have for sure. Right now, this second, this moment, this word.

Argument Two

Secondly, the present is where we will find life and living, and as we've discussed before, living, digging down deep into our life, is really what it's all about, no matter what kind of life we've picked for ourselves.

Whether our life is about learning, servitude, career, family, or some combination of these, life is what it's all about—breathing in and out, and really cherishing it.

Our human experience is happening in this very moment. We carry with us the knowledge about life and the interwoven realities we live in. But our experience of life is happening right now. Not in our memories or even in our dreams for the future, but right now. For this reason, we must focus on the present.

When I was working towards creating my own personal philosophy without realizing that was what I was doing with my life, it was easy to just be unhappy with the situation. It's easy to get unhappy when you realize you're unhappy. When this happens, you might want to forget you ever thought about confronting your dysfunction.

As a result, you could end up continuing the path you're on, living your life the way you have been. Then, before you know it, your life has gone by, the wounds are still there, and the pain never got kicked out.

Without living in the moment and without cherishing the life you have lived; you rob yourself of moments that you could spend being happy. Rather than doing that, make changes, work towards growth, healing, and greater happiness. Those are your big picture plans.

Your goal for today, in this moment, is to do at least one thing each day that matches your new personal philosophy. Do what you can to cherish the day you are living in.

- That might be sitting in a quite space by yourself with a cup of coffee and savoring each sip.
- Doing something with a loved one.
- Making a list of three things you're grateful for.
- Watching an animal, bug, or element of nature. Just to see the living proof of a loving Spirit.
- Smiling when you can.
- Breathe. Slow down your life so you can see your personal philosophy in action.

PART 3: THE HUMAN EXPERIENCE – LIFE AS I UNDERSTAND IT

Rather than choosing to be despondent, do what you can each day to find happiness. Maybe it's one thing, or two, or more; do as many things as you can each day that will help you cherish the moment you are in.

Approaching your life in this way will not only help you preserve your sanity and stay grounded, it will also give you that boost in strength to give yourself time to make those big changes.

In my personal experience, this is where you truly find happiness, because you are happy in the moment. You are cherishing life while you are still building towards more.

I don't mean "more" in the sense that what you are doing right now is worthless, but "more" in the sense that you are creating a life that is even greater than it was yesterday.

I look at where I was fifteen years ago, and life was pretty great. Ten years ago, five years ago, two years ago—each time life has become greater than I thought it could be. Sure, there have been bumps, wounds, scars, and pain, and yet overall, I have been very happy and have cherished each moment. I have healed from the wounds I encountered rather than using rotten apples to bring more into my life.

When I have encountered those tough lessons or endured those hard moments, I have had the tools to not only honor the moment, but to let them go so I could move on to that next moment.

In choosing to live in the present moment, we heal and can return to Earth, the place where our bodies and souls reside. It is from this present moment that we can choose what our lives will be like. Through these choices not only do we heal our fragmentation, but we take back our own innate power—the power to live life our way.

We end up having healed ourselves and having helped to heal the world. We have crafted a life that manifests a thriving experience available to us. Isn't life and Earth fabulous? Isn't normal an amazing adventure?

Take Away Part Three:

- Our life is made up of our internal and external reality (soul and Solar System).
- Our life is our responsibility. By taking responsibility you come into your power. You also begin to play an active role in your life. You begin to live on your terms. This is why we put the "wisdom" of the world to the test.
- In balancing these two aspects of life, we honor our own life and the community we share.
- Life is about taking all our knowledge, wisdom, and tools, and applying them to the present moment.

PART 4

Your Personal Philosophy

I've lost my way
and tonight,
I gaze upon the light you've made

to guide me home

home to where my soul awaits
home to where my soul is safe
home to where I've fought to reach
    fought to stay

the light you made
shines within the darkness
to where I lay

it reminds me of our way

shadow is where we fall
shadow is where we fight
shadow is where we learn
where we connect to light

As the world continues on its own healing journey, we as people encounter a new world. The old ways are being tested, and ancient "truths" are being eliminated. Just as these rotten apples are being purged, ancient wisdom is experiencing a re-birth. It is in this way that we as individuals and as a global community are undertaking our healing journeys.

As we choose what wisdom we will carry with us and what new wisdom we seek to learn, we create a new reality. Over the years my healing has continued, and my knowledge has grown. Yet there is much I still don't know or even understand.

But one truth that I have come to know, is the power of humanity. As a human being, I have a habit of watching people. It started years ago in an attempt to learn who I was.

In doing so, I have witnessed on multiple occasions the strength of people. To band together or stand up, no matter what challenges or pain we have faced, there exists the potential in people to shape and change reality. To acknowledge and utilize the community we share on a soul level.

The Special Truth teaches us of our value. That we are each of us, special and important, starting with our very first breath.

With this Special Truth and the responsibility we have for our own lives we learn of another truth, the truth that we hold unalienable rights. As our understanding of freedom changes and grows, we begin to see an alignment between the potential and a reality for prosperity.

Through the course of this book, I have aimed to not only teach you the importance of our personal philosophy, but also about what to do with this knowledge. I have covered philosophy and then the foundational conclusions about a human experience.

This healing journey we have started on has been building to this. To you. To how you will choose to live your life. Our dreams and desires guide our way, yet it is the knowledge that we utilize, that manifests these dreams into reality.

Our next step covers the prep work of building onto the bedrock of a human experience. In this way, we can shape a personalized human experience.

We will cover these points:
- Energy
- Your Power
- Your safety

Energy:

I started talking about energy when I spoke of Spirt transmuting raw energy into form. Now, I am going to explain just what I meant…

In philosophy, data, arguments, and conclusions are essential to the truth we know. But where I differ from most philosophers is that I believe in more than the five sense that philosophers utilize.

For you to follow along, we need to go back to my understanding of Spirit. Our loving creator.

According to my understanding and conclusions about Spirit, we've discovered that Spirit has done all Spirit can to set us up for the best possible existence. Spirit has allowed us free-will to make our own decisions and live a life in the way we choose. Not to mention not violating that free will, which I see as a great sign of respect and love.

The examples of Spirit's personality and approach to us and our human experience shows us time and time again the love, support, gifts, patience, and so much more that Spirit offers us.

Part of Spirit's gift in life is the esoteric component we can discover—esoteric being the things that our five sense can't detect. One of those unseen forces in our lives is energy.

I started to talk about energy when Spirit transmuted raw energy into a planet. While on a human level we have started to delve into the world of energy, from my perspective, science has only scratched the surface.

But science does allow us a jumping off point so that we can get our feet wet, gain a basic understanding about energy, and then delve deeper. That's what we're going to do, because energy is going to play a vital role in the practical application and understanding of reality and the tools I will introduce to you moving forward.

> ## ENERGY:
> "a fundamental entity of nature that is transferred between parts of a system in the production of physical change within the system and usually regarded as the capacity for doing work"
>
> Merriam Webster's Dictionary

Einstein provided us the equation: $E=mc^2$ to describe the relationship energy has in our lives. This equation was actually originally published as $m=E/c^2$ in order to demonstrate, in a mathematical fashion, the relationship between energy and matter, matter being the stuff we see, touch, and taste (the five senses). What Einstein's equation showed us is that matter and energy are inexplicably linked. Matter is pretty much energy.

Matter takes raw energy and defines it for us. It gives us the DNA, if you will, of energy. This DNA will determine what energy is, how it works, and what it can do. It takes pure energy and draws it into a finite thing or purpose.

When we look at the relationship matter has with energy, then at the relationship energy has with energy, we can draw conclusions that will influence our understanding of life: both of our realities and of the human experience.

> ### THE LOGICAL SERIES OF CONCLUSIONS ABOUT ENERGY:
>
> - Energy can influence energy.
>
> - We are made of matter
>
> - Because of this, Einstein's equation demonstrates to us that we are energy. A specific kind of energy.
>
> - A human body, a specific body.
>
> **Conclusion:** Because we are made of matter, we are energy. Energy influences energy, so we are influenced by energy. We also can influence other things made of energy. From these series of conclusions, we can build tools that utilize the principles of energy.

From this conclusion, we can build onto science's understanding of energy, leading us to an entire world we can become a part of. This basic understanding of energy supports us as we build and grow. It aids us in developing tools that will assist us in our healing journey, perceptions that will give us a more complete outlook on soul and Solar System, and a sense of empowerment in life.

For example:

When we look at a rock, we can apply this understanding of energy into a specific example.

- A rock is matter. We can touch it, we can taste it, we can throw it and it's going to fly, and then we can hear it thud onto the ground. This rock is made of matter, and matter is telling us what kind of energy this rock has become.
- So, if a rock is matter and matter is energy, a rock is energy.
- Energy influences energy.
- So, when we pull a crystal into our environment, we can utilize the energy of that crystal, and this is how we have crystal healing.
- Each crystal is going to have its own healing properties, because each crystal has its own DNA; its own type of matter. This is going to influence what type of energy it has, because remember, it's no longer raw energy, it is a specific kind of energy. It has been transmuted.

Moving forward we are going to look at the role energy has in our lives. As a result, we'll be able to pull in tools that are all built upon the premise of energy and utilize them to understand our lives, ourselves, helping to transform our human experience into one where we thrive.

Your Power

We have taken responsibility for the condition of our human experience. But through time and accidental or intentional neglect, we can feel that we've lost the power to control and create the life we dreamed of. We forget the power that comes when we utilize the responsibility we have for our own life.

For this reason, it is time to take our power back. To do this, we are going to utilize a new tool in our toolbox. We are going to use a visualization technique that aids you in seeing the condition of your power and retrieving all the pieces so you can be its sole owner.

Using a Visualization Technique:

Energy, while a new concept for many people, has always been an integral part of our lives. Energy has always influenced energy. When we become aware of this reality and choose to use this influence in a conscious way, we become Energy Workers.

In choosing to use visualization techniques, all we are doing is becoming those conscious Energy Workers. You merely need to read what follows and allow your mind to fill in the blanks of the image. In this way, your intuition will fill in the gaps with an accurate image of your current condition.

Then, continue reading for the next steps, to heal the seat of your power and reclaim the control you have relinquished to others during your life.

In this way you will successfully utilize this tool and reclaim your power.

Reclaiming Your Power Visualization Technique

Imagine within your mind a faucet. Rust sits within the grooves. Dust clings to the copper turned green. Underneath, the tiles appear as parched as the desert. Age has layered over the tiles for so long, you don't even know what color they are.

Past the faucet's cob-webbed opening, past the key-shaped lever, lie pipes that drive deep within you, past where your eyes seem able to see.

This faucet holds within it your power. Your energy. Your self-love.

This power resides deep within yourself. Image a deep well sitting against the base of your spine and it seems to travel deeper than the roots of the trees. Deeper than the earth's core. All the way to the center of your soul.

We seem to have allowed our power to lie dormant too long. It is time to call it forth again.

First, we must repair the damage our neglect has done. Travel with me to this well. Let's walk around the well and push the stone walls back together. Gather the soil at its base into your hand. With your other hand, reach deep within the well and call your power to you. Mix your power and the soil, create a paste. Fill the holes of your well.

There seem to be these plastic pipes jammed into the sides of your well. They travel farther than your eyes can see. We must remove them. It is time to take back your power from others.

We can choose to defer to others with more knowledge. We might not mind when they take charge, but they may not have our power.

Pull the plastic pipes, see how easily they slip away. They seem to travel past your line of sight. Retracting and returning to its owner. They may keep their pipes.

Walk around your well and see that all the pipes are gone.

- See that the walls stand tall.
- See that the holes no longer exist.

Then dip both hands into the well and speak with me-
"Forgive me for my neglect. Please come to me. Fill the brim of my well, see how strong and tall it stands. Come home."

As your power flows up within the well's wall we must reattach our pipe. Our copper pipe has fallen off to the side. Pick it up and look at it within your hands. It is green with age. It is bent.

But we can straighten it. We can bring it back to life. Caress the length of your pipe within your hands; send the pipe your love. This pipe will carry your power from the source of your soul until it reaches your human form, until you can manifest it out into the world.

See how straight it holds itself now? Twist it into the side of the well where it belongs. Now see it grow as it twists about you, past you, until it reaches once more our faucet.

Come back to your faucet with me. Turn the key and let a drop fall out into your hands. Take your power and wipe the faucet. See how it gleams now. Brighter than before, stronger, wiser.

Now, twist the key again until drops slip past the mouth of the faucet and spread against the ground.
But it is not ground, it is not even tile. Hmm. It is me.

My power is dripping into me. Filling me with all I can be.
The power to decide what my life is like. This power resides within me. This power fills me. This power will never run dry. And when I feel my power is not enough, I have a direct link to the divine. To my guides. To life itself.
And my power is SO strong that I only need it to drop, to drip.

    Drip
        Drip
           Drip
              Drip

When my days run long and others attempt to take my power away, I can turn the key of my faucet within my mind and spread energy and power throughout my blood stream. For this is my power.

After the moment has passed, I turn the key, return to my drips of power, and sleep to rejuvenate myself.

The power inside you is yours. What you do with it, where you allocate it, is up to you. Whether you use your power to try new things, to lead, to take charge, to change, to heal, to create or to destroy, is all up to you.

Sometimes we don't know our own power because we gave it away a long time ago. It is time to find it and take it back. There will still be moments where you can choose to follow others, let others call the shots. But only when it is good for you. Only when their control comes from your powerful decision to give it to them, and only for as long as you say.

With your power restored, consider these questions:

- Has your power been neglected?
- How have you been using/not using your power?
- Now that you have your power, where/how might you use it?

How are you feeling? I am so proud of you. As one who has read this book many times in the process of writing, editing, and publishing it, I know from experience that I've covered a lot. You've learned so much.

Take a moment and celebrate all you've accomplished. Take that minute and just breathe.

In….

Feel your lungs expanding. Positive, healing, and loving energy traveling from the air into your body.

Out…

Feel your power pulsing, expelling the air and toxic energy within your body out into the world. Let your power soothe this energy so that as it leaves your body, negativity leaves, and healing energy enters the world.

Breathe with me for a minute. Set that timer for a minute and celebrate your importance. Rejoice in the Special Truth of who you are.

The Six Safety Tools

Before I leave you, I want to share with you some tools you can start utilizing today. In life we encounter many twists and turns. The nature of these twists is created when we choose a course of action, a path of happiness or pain.

These twists and turns can manifest positive or negative energy. When we choose to clean up our life, we may encounter dirt, dysfunction, and debris. To stay safe, I use my Six Safety Tools.

Over the years and through the course of my learning, I have discovered these tools and consider them a vital part of my daily life. What's so great about these tools, is that you can start utilizing them today. Moving forward, life is going to get a little rocky. We're going to be throwing everything in our basket onto the ground and start making some changes.

This is when great transformation and change happens. This is also when some of those crazy, question-my-sanity moments occur. There are even moments where we might experience depression and aggression as we reevaluate our life and ourselves, especially since we won't be running away from any aspect of who we are.

Before we get into that, I want to set you up for a strong healing journey and a strong life. I cannot take away potential pain or confusion, but I can help set you up for the smoothest transformation, or rebirth, possible.

The way I can do this is to supply you with some energy tools that you can utilize every single day, even multiple times a day, to help influence the result of your day and this journey. These will help you stay safe not only on a physical level, but a mental, emotion, and spiritual level, as well.

Grounding

Our life, as we have come to learn, is comprised of many different components. When we weave them together in a healthy way, we achieve a thriving human experience. But not every aspect of our lives is within our power of control.

We encounter people, places, things, and the unknown, all of which can influence the quality of our lives in positive and negative ways. One way we can mitigate the potential for upheaval and worry is to use the tool known as Grounding.

> ### GROUNDING:
> "The use of energy to connect you with the Earth, helping to keep you safe."

As you can see, we are going to build onto your understanding and use of energy. Grounding, like some of the other safety tools, is built upon the foundation of energy.

We as Energy Workers are going to consciously use our ability to influence energy with the specific purpose of grounding. This time we will do so using a visualization technique (just like we did when you reclaimed your power).

How Does Grounding Work?

Grounding and other visual techniques work for a number of reasons. Not only is energy work involved, but we are accomplishing other things, as well.

This grounding technique not only manipulates energy but stimulates a mental transition for you. When using a visualization technique, you are shifting the reality of your perception within your mind.

Your mind is a powerful tool and due to this has the ability to consciously transform what type of energy there is within you and around you. It also changes your perception. When you ground yourself, you are changing how your brain understands the situation so that you can feel relaxed as opposed to stressed.

Lastly, this tool works because in the course of shifting energy, you will be connecting with Mother Earth and the Solar System. This energetic connection supports you as a human being, consciously weaving you into the external world in a healthy and safe way.

When to Use Grounding

- When the business of the modern world pulls.
- When we are working within ourselves.
- When we are emotional and so much is happening.
- When we can't feel the ground.
- When we feel like we need to hang on for safety.

The Grounding Technique is Great Because

- It can be done by anyone.
- It can be done anywhere.
- It can be adapted to work the best for you.

How to Ground: The Visualization for Grounding

Plant your feet on the floor (whether you're standing or sitting). Close your eyes and visualize a great big oak tree. Imagine the massive root system starting at your feet and sinking deep within the Earth, connecting you to the world.

Just as the root system keeps the tree upright, so too will these roots. Take a moment to marvel in the strength you've found in gaining aid from the earth. Just as a tree is at home, you as a human being are, too.

Spend some time just enjoying the sensation of being grounded. Even as the moment ends and your consciousness returns to the tasks at hand, this connection remains.

ALTERNATIVE IMAGES

For some people, the image of a root system doesn't jive within their mind. As an alternative, these are some other visualizations you can create to connect and ground:

• An anchor and chain: As before, plant your feet, then allow the chain to flow past your feet and deep into the ocean, where the anchor can land upon the ocean floor.

• The locking mechanism of trains to their track: I like this image when I want to ground but am moving around a lot. Since roots are stationary, it doesn't always fit within my mind. In this way, you can chug around your home, getting all you need done while also remaining fastened to the earth.

• A mountain: Imagine the heaviness of this mountain planting you into the earth. No matter the height in which you travel or the force of those who wish to unsettle you, you are still this mountain anchored into the earth, connected and grounded.

You can come up with your own image, as well.
Use whatever speaks to you.

*If the visualization doesn't seem to work for you, you can ask your spirit guides for aid. You can also move your arms and hands as you work through the visualization, grounding the practice a bit more.

> ### HOW TO STRENGTHEN YOUR GROUNDING
>
> Grounding is a visualization technique and utilizes your imagination and your connection to what you imagine. The stronger your connection and image, the stronger the power. Here are some techniques for strengthening your grounding:
>
> - Stand upon the earth in bare feet.
> - Pair this tool with a grounding crystal stone.

Build Upon Grounding

With this simple visualization, we can ground. But if you want to take the next step as Energy Workers, you can add to this simple visualization and do more than just ground.

We Can Detox

Once you have the image of your tree settled within your mind, call on your spirit guides to aid you in removing the negative energy within your body. Then imagine energy flowing from the earth into the roots of your tree and up into your being.

This energy is of a healing nature, often described as white, golden (like in Reiki), or purple. As you imagine this loving energy flowing up into your being, it cascades over your head and heads back to your roots; into the earth, bringing with it all the negativity it can find within your body.

As this energy enters the earth, your spirit guides transmute this energy from a negative force into a healing one. Not only will you be rid of this negativity, but the earth will discover new healing energy.

Sit with this exercise and bring healing energy into your being as many times as you need.

Another Form of Detoxifying

I learned this technique from my crystal teacher. After she had us ground with our tree, she talked us through the healing energy that would enter our body and brought up the fact that sometimes negative energy can be especially stuck; that even when we imagine the negative energy leaving us, our intuition lets us know it didn't budge.

When this happens, call on your spirit guides to form a circle around you, and as healing energy enters through your roots, ask them to hold magnets around your body. These magnets will pull the negativity out of your body, through your pores, and into the world. Once purged, this negativity will transform into healing energy for the world.

A NEW APPLE- YOUR SPIRIT GUIDES:

We have yet to talk about our spirit guides. I briefly included them when we talked about the different types of guidance Spirit has provided us, but I want to address them specifically now.

Spirit guides are souls, angels, ancestors, animals, fairies, and various other beings who spend their time with us in an energetic or unseen way. Their purpose at this time is to be our guides, teachers, and healers.

Utilizing not only their own skills to help us but also insight from our Soul Contract to help us on our journey. Spirit guides are in a unique position to not only offer us support and love but are able to take that step back from the human experience and see and understand the bigger picture.

My Conclusion:

Calling on your spirit guides does not take them away from anyone else. They are here for you and loved to be called on.

Arguments:

Just as Spirit can connect with each one of us, so can our spirit guides. They are sent to us for our life, or for portions of our journey. Just as Spirit won't violate our free will, neither will our spirit guides. This means that we must call on them for aid. In doing so, not only do those who love us get to fulfill their desire to help, but we will also reduce the struggle of life and enjoy another moment filled with happiness.

Healing

Part of the detoxifying technique includes pulling healing energy into our bodies. In this part, the focus revolves around removing the negativity. But there is another form of energy that is detrimental to our wellbeing. This is stagnant energy.

My energy healer taught me that when we experience a self-inflicted ailment, it can be a direct result of energy that has become stagnant in our body. Rather than flowing as energy normally does, this energy stays trapped and impacts our physical wellbeing.

When you experience an ailment, you can start with a simple grounding and then pull healing energy into your body. But rather than having this energy circulate your body, gathering the negativity, you can have it pool into the spaces of your body that hurt.

After letting this pool saturate into your surrounding skin/muscle/bone, visualize the healing energy pulling this stagnant energy with it as it leaves your body and travels back into the earth.

This technique does not replace herbs/medication/or a doctor's visit, but merely acts as an added aid in your recovery.

> As you remove the negativity or stagnant energy, you might feel pressure in certain areas of your body. This is a good sign. When this happens, it is your intuition/body registering the movement of energy that has been clogging you up. This slow movement just lets you know how stuck it was, and I recommend focusing on your breathing until the pressure dissipates.

Using Grounding as A Warm-Up:

As you have seen, the original grounding visualization has acted as a starting point for some other wonderful visualization techniques. Grounding is often used in conjunction with other tools we have yet to cover.

These include but are not limited to:

- The other Six Safety Tools
- Chakras
- Self-Love Ritual
- Meditation
- Energy Healing

Grounding is a wonderful tool that you can use each day to help ensure a wonderful life.

Here are some questions to consider:

- What does your visualization look like?
- When might you practice this visualization?
- How has this visualization worked for you?
- How might you alter it to make it better for you?

Feeling silly is a completely natural and acceptable response when you first start using this tool. If this happens for you, see this as an opportunity to handle the situation from a place of self-love rather than self-hate. If you need to, keep this tool private until you feel comfortable sharing it with others. As time passes, you'll find that this tool becomes just a natural part of your day.

Shielding

When we take the time to consider the ramifications of energy in our lives, we come away with the realization that anything can impact anything. I am energy, you are energy, we impact each other. When you realize this great truth, you will also realize that there are people and places in your life that you don't want to be impacted by.

We might not connect with these people or places on a physical level, but on an energetic level, we are connecting. So, shielding is a great way to mitigate and influence energy before it ever reaches us. Then, if a person chooses to send hateful energy our way consciously or subconsciously, we'll be able to turn away or transmute that energy before it even reaches us.

Think about it: we do a lot to demonstrate self-love. We lock our doors, set our alarms, and maybe even take self-defense classes. Shielding can become just one more component to your self-love practice. The bottom line is that we don't need to be unsafe. Before you even exit the door, enter the past, or address the rotten apples. If you are shielded the dysfunction doesn't have a means to reach you.

SHIELDING:

"The energy shields we construct around ourselves to protect, heal, and ease our way in life."

The Shielding Technique is Great Because

- It can be done by anyone.
- It can be done anywhere.

It can be adapted to work the best for you.

How Shielding Works:

Shielding is another visualization technique. Within our mind we construct an image that directs the energy in our lives. In this way, we are the conscious Energy Workers in the world. As always, the stronger your visualization, the stronger your energetic impact. This means that you will have the most success when you connect with the image, so change or modify it anyway you need to in order to be successful. (Take the apple that works for you.)

When to Shield

I like to ground and shielding when I first wake up. This way I have taken care of my safety before the day speeds away and I forget to do so. That being said, I also check and reapply my shield during the day when the need arises.

We're going to get into how to shield next, but part of shielding is the number of shields we use. On an average day I have two shields. But when I am encountering a difficult environment, toxic person, unhealthy situation, long day, or practicing energy healing, I add layers to fit my needs.

Since we can shield anywhere, at any time, you can call upon your shields and even re-ground yourself for support. This will help whatever moment you are in to have the greatest potential for prosperity.

How to Shield

Take a moment to ground, then close your eyes as we begin our shielding visualization technique. (As your skill increases, you won't need to ground first to be successful. But it's still a wonderful tool to use in conjunction with shielding).

Visualize with me an orb, almost like the Good Witch's bubble from the Wizard of Oz. Starting at your feet, watch as this orb glides upwards until its sides meet at the top of your head.

The orb will not pop. It flows with energy. Now, the type of energy it flows with is up to you. Different types of energy will provide you with different styles of shields, protecting you from different energies.

I was taught to start with an orb of light. This light is divine/angelic light, straight from Spirit. It protects me from the negativity of the world and keeps me safe, calm, and centered.

Afterwards you can add any number of orbs depending on the day or situation/moment you are entering. Add orbs made of…

- Energy- Love/Healing/Strength/Patience/etc.
- Crystals
- Emotions
- Colors- (can tie with your chakras)
- & more. It's all up to your imagination.

Each layer to your shield is created by what you desire, see, and feel. From that point I layer more shields onto my bubble, spreading outwards.

The Rainbow Shield

When you are finished with your shields there is one more to add onto the outskirts. This shield is made of swirling rainbows, vibrant and constant. These rainbows have a special ability—they ease your way through life.

How do they do this? Well, your rainbow shield will fluoresce at different wavelengths (colors) depending on the people you're around and environment you're in. These different wavelengths shine on different aspects of our personality, pointing out the similarities we share with those around us.

In doing so, this shield helps people to acknowledge the interwoven nature of reality. Rather than clashing with others, this shield provides us an opportunity for a connection on neutral ground.

Of course, depending on what we do or say, we can turn this neutral ground into a war zone. The rainbow shield only gives us an opportunity to connect with those around us.

With your rainbow shield in place, you are prepared to exit the door and enter the world safe and sound. As you move through life, these shields flow around your body. Their energy flows and moves with you, going with you wherever your human experience might take you.

ENERGY DRAIN:

In becoming a conscious Energy Worker your energy distribution will shift. While you have always been influencing energy, it has often been to a lesser degree.

Now that you are grounding, shielding, and more, you are expelling a small amount of energy. While the expense is less than what it costs to be around toxic people without your safety tools, how your energy is used each day will change.

At the start it might take more energy to learn how to visualize the energy you are transmuting, but through time it will settle within your mind with a snap of your fingers.

Keep this in mind when you become tired. Honor what you feel and how things are. Rather than choosing to combat the situation (rotten apple), embrace self-love and honor the truth of how you feel.

Questions to Consider:

- What sort of layers might you use?
- When might you pull up/check on/reinforce your shield?
- How has this tool worked for you?
- How might you alter shielding to work better for you?

Cutting Cords:

As we have learned, we exist in two realities: our internal world and the external one that we share. Part of our lives take place in this external world, as we experience new adventures, read new books, listen to music, and interact with people. Our interactions create doorways where cords connect us to one another. In this way we create an energetic connection.

But when the connection has ended and we both walk away, the cord remains. As a result, we can clog, influence, and even drain our energy. To clear our energy field or our subtle body, as it is commonly called, we must utilize the tool cutting cords.

> SUBTLE BODY:
> "Layers of various energy that create the interwoven energy system of our multi-dimensional being."

Why We Want to Cut Cords

Imagine, if you will, your phone or other electronic device. What sort of activities do you use this device for? Do you work, connect with people, play games?

Just as all of these interactions happen on our electronic device, so do our connections in life. And just like this electronic device, we run slower when we leave all these apps pulled up.

To maintain the healthiest existence, we need to cut these cords after each encounter in order to renew ourselves. How many connections/conversations/hugs have you had in your lifetime? Can you imagine that many cords coming off your body and stretching out into the world to other people?

Part of a thriving human experience is embracing the people we encounter and connecting with them. In this way we are digging deeply into life. Another part is making choices that help us remain safe and healthy. This is why we need to cut cords.

Unfortunately, there are times when these cords (old and new) connect us with toxic people who can drag energy from us or imbue us with the same toxic energy. Most often these people do so subconsciously, but other times they are fully aware of what they are doing (energy vampires).

Other times, we have unknowingly or knowingly been the ones to take energy or imbue others with different types of energy. But we don't need to roll over and take this abuse. We can cut the cords we have created and know safety, healing, and newfound energy.

When to Cut Cords

With each new moment we experience a new connection. This can be wonderful and beautiful. Then, as the moment passes, we can cut the cord that connects us, for both our sakes.

For this reason, I like to cut cords in the morning as part of my morning routine, as well as in the evening. This way, I wipe the slate clean for a new and fresh day.

I have also used this tool during the day, when I encounter toxic people or situations. The cutting of this cord happens during the toxic interaction, afterwards, and even sometimes as I get re-agitated when I recount my day.

Just like grounding and shielding, this tool can be used at anytime and anywhere.

How to Cut Cords

As with grounding and shielding, this tool is based on energy and the visualization technique. For this reason, I recommend starting with your grounding and shielding, then closing your eyes.

Picture in your mind's eye all the cords from all your encounters. It is time to close them all. To do this you can…

- Snip them with your gardening shears.
- Pull the plug.
- Swipe them away.
- Cut the cord, cut the string, and watch it zip back into the universe.
- Let go of the slinky.

Sit with this visualization until all doorways are closed and all cords are gone. Get rid of the ones you have created, and the ones others have. In this way you are hitting the refresh button.

If this is your first time cutting cords, you might need to sit with this visualization for a time. If you grow tired, call a quits for the day and tomorrow do another deep cleaning.

If you have worked with an Energy Healer, they may have cleared your energy field already. The more consistently you use this tool, the more impact and greater effect it will have. Not only will you be able to pull this image up within your mind at any time, but you will have less cords to snip away, thus requiring less energy to maintain a healthy energy field.

Consider These Questions:

- How might you visualize this tool?
- When might you use this tool?
- How effective has this tool been for you?
- How might you alter, or add to this tool for it to be more effective for you?

"Bless me, Bless you"

In life we are successful when we integrate Soul and Solar System. That's when we take into consideration our responsibility to the external world, our relationship with the external world, and the external world's impact. One of the big life lessons is learning how to keep ourselves safe, healthy, and happy without rejecting components of the external world.

When we reject something, we not only fixate on that thing (using our energy to shove it away), but we spend a moment in our life not experiencing love, healing, or happiness. Instead, we spend a moment expelling energy and feeling something akin to fear or anger.

Yet at the same time, we don't want to take on things that aren't good for us, be they energy, advice, or opinions. So, how do we not accept these things and still spend a moment of our life experiencing happiness?

This is where our "Bless me, bless you" tool comes in handy.

What others may offer that we don't want:

Sometimes these things come from loved ones attempting to aid us. Other times, they come from toxic people wishing to spread their pain or manipulate us…

- Unhealthy advice.
- Dysfunctional thinking or points of view.
- Unhealthy opportunities.
- Negative or toxic energy.

How This Tool Works

Like the other three Safety Tools, here, we are utilizing energy. The difference is that this is not only a visualization technique, but a physical one. Through the use of your body, you will influence the energy around you, bringing good things your way (not what you wished to decline) and sending good energy back out into the world (thus, not harming others).

When To Use This Tool?

The beauty of this tool is that anyone can use it and it can be used anywhere. For these reasons, you can utilize this tool during a difficult situation where someone wishes to share with you something you don't want (be that energy or something physical).

With this tool you can decline negative energy and bolster your own strength to honor and enforce your boundaries. This will help you to honor your needs and choices.

Lastly, you can use this tool when you are recounting a difficult moment, considering a difficult person, or at any other time you feel the need.

How to Use This Tool

Mentally or verbally say, "Bless me," and bring your hands towards you. As you bring your hands closer, part your fingers and imagine as if your fingers are a rake, selecting only that which is good for you and pulling it closer.

Then, once your hands reach your body (mine are generally near my stomach), rotate them so they face outwards and rake them away, saying, "bless you."

In this manner, you are raking away that which is not good for you (transmuting the energy into healing/loving energy) and sending good things to others. This mental and physical act sends out our intentions, which influence our environment and interactions.

Consider These Questions:

- When might you use this tool?
- What have you discovered in using this tool?
- What might you alter, add, or reduce to make this tool more effective for you?

Incense & Smudging

This fifth safety tool diverts from the ones I've already introduced in that it utilizes tools found within the physical world. Incense and smudging are going to influence your subtle body and your environment, as well. This physical, mental, and energetic influence makes incense a potent tool, not to mention the influence incense and smudging have on your environment.

We retain the energy we are exposed to unless we shield from it or purge it. As a result, our environment bares the energetic markings of what has happened. But with incense, we can not only clear the energy within us, but around us, as well.

How Does Incense Work?

This wonderful tool works on a few different levels. The first level is a mental one. Incense give off specific scents depending on the herbs, plants, and/or wood that is used. What you may not know is that of all our senses, our sense of smell is directly wired to your brain.

Due to this, incense provides a quick connection to your brain for immediate impact. This means that if we burn an incense each day we come home, we learn to associate this smell with a sense of peace and safety.

Secondly, while we enjoy the smell, our body changes, as well. A physiological response is triggered when we burn certain incense, causing a biochemical reaction.

Lastly, this tool influences the nature of energy within us and in our environment, providing an overall mental, physical, and energetic influence.

When to Use Incense:

There are many ways we can use this multifaceted tool. We can clear our energy, our environment's energy, and even clear the energy of other tools we use (i.e., crystals and tarot). Incense can even become a part of our other spiritual activities, such as meditations or rituals.

Incense can also be used to improve our mood when we're angry, hurt, or have had a bad day. Lastly, incense work well in covering bad smells (like dog farts). Essentially, you can use this tool at any time, for whatever need you have.

The Components of Incense & Smudging

In order to utilize this tool, you will need two things: incense and an incense holder.

The Types of Incense

- Joss Sticks, Cylinders, & Cones: This incense will burn completely.
- Masala Sticks: These incense don't burn completely. What will be left at the end is the stick. (These are commonly seen in movies.)
- Loose incense: These burn completely.

> **BEWARE SYNTHETIC INCENSE:**
> When choosing which brand of incense to purchase, avoid the incense made of synthetic materials. Not only do you not know what they are made of, but you lose the physiological impact and achieve a diminished energetic influence.
>
> Because of this reason my family buys from Juniper Ridge. Not only do they have a wide range of options, but we can buy in large quantities since we use our incense daily.

The Types of Incense Burner/Holder

- Boats: Often wooden or ceramic, these incense burners appear flat, with a curved end and a small hole. They hold masala sticks and are the most widely available of all the types of burners. (They can also be made of soapstone, glass, metal, or clay.)
- Trees: These are the wooden holders with many holes on top. They are used for masala sticks. While boats hold single incense horizontally, trees can hold many sticks vertically.
- Combination burners: Generally, soapstone or ceramic, these burners have a section for every type of incense imaginable.
- Censers: These holders are used for a more specialized incense. These bowls hold ash or sand to cradle the incense and provide a fireproof base for incense that burn completely. (They are often used by tarot readers and Energy Healers.)

How to Get Started

When initially starting with this tool, your first step is to purchase an incense burner and your incense. Most esoteric or metaphysical shops sell them. You can also find them online. I recently saw incense at Rite Aid. Imagine that!

Next, you want to consider where you are getting your incense. It's super important to avoid synthetic materials. When we want to clear energy and impact the energy around us, synthetic will not aid our purpose.

After you have your materials, you're ready to get started.

Burning Your Incense

Step One: Choose a safe place in your home for your incense, away from curtains, high traffic zones, and windows (or other places where the embers might blow off your holder).

Step Two: Place your incense onto or in your holder.

Step Three: Light your incense, exposing the incense to the flame for 5-10 seconds.

Step Four: Enjoy!

BURNING TIPS:

Fire to ember

The flame on most incense will burn out on their own in a few seconds and be reduced to just a burning ember that smokes. However, if the incense does not go out within a few seconds, you will need to blow it out.

10–20 seconds

When you first light your incense, it will take 10-20 seconds before the burning smoke will clear and you'll smell the actual scent.

Upside down

For cone incense, getting them to catch can be difficult. If a cone incense refuses to light, then turn the cone upside down and light the wide end first.

Fan or Feather

You can use a fan or feather to direct the smoke of the incense. This can be done as part of a ritual or to help the smoke reach the corners of your home as you cleanse your house.

PART 4: YOUR PERSONAL PHILOSOPHY

Making Your Own Incense:

I recently came across a book all about it. Before that time, I didn't know you could make your own. If you are interested in crafting your own- check out this book: *Incense - Crafting & Use of Magickal Scents*, by: Carl F. Neal

If you are merely interested in learning more about incense, check out *Incense and Incense Ritual*, by: Thomas Kinkele.

Smudging

Smudging, while slightly different than using incense, falls under this category because you are burning something in your space. Smudging acts as a heavy-duty cleansing of your home and self.

How Do You Smudge?

Step One: Most commonly, smudging is done with a stock of sage. (Rosemary and thyme are also used.)

Step Two: Light the stock of sage. If you're having a difficult time, change the angle of the sage. Sometimes turning it upside down (hanging over the match) is more effective.

Step Three: Once your stock is burning with some embers (it's uncommon to get the entire top to burn), walk about your home directing the smoke. You can do this with a fan, feather, or even your hand.

To smudge yourself, merely move it around your body at a safe distance. You can smudge as part of a self-love ritual, or as part of your monthly house cleaning. You can also sing or pray as you move from room to room.

Step Four: To put out your stock of sage (it will last you a while) you have a few choices. You can dip the end in water (though it requires time to dry out), you can leave it to burn out in a bowl (which doesn't always work), or you can take a blade and knock off the burning pieces of sage.

Consider These Questions:

- Why type of incense might you use?
- Where might you use it?
- When will your burn your incense?

The Elements

This final tool takes us back to our connection with the Solar System. Through the course of this book, we have learned just how we weave into the world. In this case I am not talking about weaving with fellow souls, but with Mother Earth.

As human beings, we are linked to our home, this planet. Just as we influence her condition, she influences ours. We can utilize this influence and embrace Mother Earth's various forms to imbue our bodies with healing, love, and happiness.

How to Use the Elements

The five elements can be used in various forms to fit our needs, environments, and time. This first form is the elements themselves: earth, fire, water, air, or metal. If the element is not available or safe, we can pull the energy of this element from the image, color, or sound.

Examples of Utilizing the Elements

Water: Water cleanses and acts as an insulator.

- A simple shower can cleanse your body, and the water around you can create a shield from the world. With water, you can purge what you no longer need. Often, water can create a quiet space so the messages from our spirit guides can come through.
- Install a water feature. It moves energy and allows for energy to pool.
- Dancing in the rain can be a moment of joy. As well as listening to rain sounds when going to sleep.
- Don't forget that drinking water works well, too, flushing toxins and refreshing your body.

Fire: From destruction to rebirth, fire is a mighty force. Like a phoenix rising from the ashes, you can use fire to symbolically or literally burn away toxins to bring about a rebirth.

- Light a candle. You can also pair this with the tool of essential oils, specific herbs, or crystals for added benefit.
- Burn an incense.
- Burn away connections (to people and things). Write what you want to burn on a piece of paper and set it to flames. (Just make sure you are doing in a safe environment, ideally outside in a wide-open space, and watch you don't burn your fingers).
- You can also stand or sit in front of a fireplace and experience the flame's heat brush against your body, removing all toxins and warming your very core, building a reserve of strength.

- You can paint a red border around your door, so every time you come and walk through the door, the fire's energy will burn away the remnants of the day.

Earth: Getting back out into nature after a hard day does wonders.

- Sit outside and soak up the sun's rays. Half an hour of sunshine provides you with needed vitamin D.
- Garden or walk barefoot on the earth.
- I understand that not everyone lives where nature resides. If that is the case, having potted plants does wonders too.
- Remember that earth colors work well, too. Deep browns and greens will act as a grounding energy to link you back to Earth. Your grounding technique pulls in the Earth's energy, as well.
- A lose leaf tea also works wonders. From the water component, to Earth's own plants, you incorporate the elements of both earth and water.
  - If you choose to sweeten it, use honey, preferably local. Honey helps to aid your body in guarding against potential local allergies.

Air: From the air we breathe to the wind's ability to shift energies, we can do a lot to cleanse ourselves with the element of air.

- Try deep breathing exercises.
- We can also take a feather or a fan and create wind to shift the energies around us.
- Open windows.

- Dancing can stimulate air to move and shift energies. (Think more spinning and less twerking.)
- Fabric choice may vary. Choose to wear fabrics that let air flow freely. Choose a blue like the sky, or a white or clear fabric. You can also select a fabric with the image of a tree, with wind moving the limbs.

Metal: In Feng Shui, metal breaks up earth much like a farmer's plow; it also chops wood, like an ax. You can use metal in your personal practice to break up the monotony or stuck energies.

- Try wearing various metal jewelry.
- A wind chime does wonders. (Sound is also great at releasing energies. The vibrations from sound interacts with your own personal vibrations, shifting them).
- Consider using a metal fan. You'll combine the cleansing elements of both air and metal.

Consider These Questions

- Which of these tools might you try?
- When might you use them?
- What other ideas or adjustments might you implement to make these tools better for you?
- Do you know of any more tools that might work well?

> **ON THE GO RE-CAP:**
>
> On my website: **http://raemedicinewoman.com** you'll find articles covering each of these Six Safety Tools. If you need to refresh your mind, you can access this information at anytime, anywhere.

With that, I have taught you my Six Safety Tools. Woven into my daily life, they aid me each day. As with everything else I have shared with you, I encourage you to challenge what you've read in this section and take only what works best for you.

Take Away Part Four:

- Energy is woven into the reality of the world.
- Energy influences our lives.
- As beings made of energy, we are influenced and can influence life.
- We can utilize visualization techniques to reclaim our power and to stay safe.

EPILOGUE:

There was a time when I was a young girl in pain. I was lost to even myself as I strove to learn how to live my life. For that reason, I started a healing journey that not only changed my way of life but helped me heal from trauma I sustained long ago.

Within this volume, we started out on a healing journey that will build to a thriving life. With new wisdom and a strong bedrock in place, you have accomplished a great and deep level of healing. Take a moment to smile and acknowledge your strength to stop, turn around, and face your dysfunction in the eye.

Your healing journey continues, with each day you choose healthy apples, perceptions, and actions. In this manner, your healing will build upon itself, growing and bringing you to new heights.

As I've said before, you do not walk this path alone, and you are not required to take anything that does not benefit you. Become belief contingent with me. Question the world, what you know, and what you encounter. Help me to leave rotten apples on the Earth to decompose.

For me, for you, and for all of us. Let us improve the human experience. To align ourselves with the possibilities and prosperity that isn't just possible in our dreams but in reality too.

ABOUT THE AUTHOR

Rae Beecher is an empath, energy healer, tarot reader, and medicine woman. With her debut book, she has compiled her knowledge about a healthy, happy, and prosperous life, to share with the world. Having studied with healers and spent a year soaking up the wisdom of a great tarot reader, she developed her own understanding of life, while learning the skills necessary to help others do the same.

www.ingramcontent.com/pod-product-compliance
Lightning Source LLC
LaVergne TN
LVHW091553060526
838200LV00036B/815